How to Write a Screenplay in 10 Weeks –
The Horowitz System®

By Marilyn Horowitz

Other books by Marilyn Horowitz:

How to Write a Screenplay Using the Horowitz System® – The High School Edition
Copyright © 2008 by Marilyn Horowitz

How to Write a Screenplay Using the Horowitz System® – The Middle School Edition
Copyright © 2008 by Marilyn Horowitz

How to Write a Screenplay Using the Horowitz System® – The Middle School Edition: Film Breakdowns Supplement
Copyright © 2009 by Marilyn Horowitz

The Four Magic Questions of Screenwriting: Structure Your Screenplay Fast
Copyright © 2009 by Marilyn Horowitz

The Four Magic Questions of Screenwriting – Student Workbook
Copyright © 2010 by Marilyn Horowitz

Introduction

Dear Fellow Writers:

The Horowitz System® is a precise system of exercises and processes that when done in order allows you to write fast and efficiently. The system works because it excites both the analytic "left" brain and the intuitive "right" brain. What is unique about this system is that, contrary to the notion that intuition is random or haphazard, it will teach you to harness your intuition and summon it at will. This will allow you to pre-visualize your screenplay in a new way. Another benefit of using the System® is that it's been designed to help each student perfect his or her own individual creative process. My intention is to help every writer reconnect with his or her natural brilliance. If you've previously been introduced my writing system via The Four Magic Questions, you will find that the additional techniques in this book will help you to become a master of screenwriting.

The effect of the System® is cumulative, and you must do the work exactly as it is assigned. This will require you to make a leap of faith, since the arrangement of the book is not in a traditional linear order, but rather is designed with an understanding of how these different parts of the brain function. You will often be asked to work with a timer. Try it out; you will see how helpful working fast can be. However, only you can actually do the writing. When writing a first draft it is important to remember that the golden key is "Don't get it right—get it written." After you've completed the prep work in Steps 1–4, just start putting words on the page, and **in 10 weeks you will have written a screenplay.**

Good luck and happy writing.

Table of Contents

How to Use The Horowitz System®

How to Use the Horowitz System®

The Horowitz System® has been designed to allow you to write your story exactly as you see it in your imagination, so you will create something that is unique and original. The System also trains you to express your vision using an industry standard form, the three-act structure, which guarantees that your screenplay will be easier to sell. Developing, writing or rewriting screenplays this way is fun and will require fewer revisions because you've learned an extremely efficient type of preparation. You actually "see" your screenplay before you write it.

The **first step** in The System is to create an imaginary life for your characters, and to do that you must understand what they want. The initial set of exercises will help you visualize your characters in a personal, experiential way because you will use yourself as a reference point. By exposing yourself to certain information, you can gauge your own responses and then compare them to those of your characters. By understanding how your characters will respond in a specific, action-oriented way, you can elicit the story through their behavior, rather than making it up.

The **second step** is to **determine your Premise-Question.** A premise is a statement that describes the underlying reasons for writing a story, such as "Good overcomes Evil." By formulating this statement you connect with the point of your story. By turning that statement into a question, "Does Good overcome Evil?," your writing will be compelling because you are exploring a question rather than proving a point. A new screenplay is best built from the Premise-Question forward, with correctly motivated characters so the plot rises from conflict to crisis with ease.

The **third step** is to **re-examine your main characters in terms of the Premise-Question.** The goal is to understand and/or intuit why your hero or heroine is the only character who can star in your script. Only by connecting the plot's Premise-Question with your character's goal can you build the rock-solid foundation needed for a strong first draft.

The **fourth step** is to **plot your screenplay.** The core of **The Horowitz System®** is *the Mythic Journey Map*, which provides a new and simpler way of understanding film plot and structure.

The **fifth step** is **to write your screenplay in 10 weeks.** Use the timeline and log to organize your time. Remember: "Don't get it right—get it written."

The **final step** is to **make sure your script is professionally presented** using the *Spec-Script Format Guide*.

STEP 1
CHARACTER
Creating Your Characters

Step 1

Creating Your Characters – Exercises

Yourself

Exercises A – G

Yourself: Exercise A

Whenever you create, start with yourself first. Using yourself as if you were going to be a character in your own screenplay will help you to have a clear basis for comparison when building your other characters.

A. **Draw your family.** Put yourself in the drawing. Select a symbolic object for each member, such as a hat or a baseball bat for a little boy or a bone for a dog. This is not about drawing ability; it is to help you visualize better.

Yourself: Exercise B

B. Describe a **formative event** in childhood that could explain why you do what you do—
    what drives and motivates you. Understanding what drives you will make it easier for
    you to understand what drives your characters.

Yourself: Exercise C

C.   Most of us receive conflicting **"messages"** from our parents or other adults about how to be when we grow up. For example, "Don't make waves," "Fight for what you want," etc. What were they for you? How did you reconcile them? Most people either want to please or rebel. How did you choose to react? Knowing this will help you do the next exercise.

Yourself: Exercise D

D. **Define the "spine."** "Spine" is an acting term that is used to mean one of the following: "who you are," "what you most want out of life" and/or your "reason for being." Most inner conflicts arise from trying to please yourself or others at the same time. If you can locate your own inner conflict, it will be easier to find it in your characters. Inner conflict is defined as what is inside you that is preventing you from achieving your goal. Finding inner conflict is the spark that will start the fire of your script.

Yourself: Exercises E – G

E.   Write a short paragraph about **atoning** for doing something wrong.

F.   Write a short paragraph describing being wronged and wanting **revenge.**

G.   Write a short paragraph about dealing with **unrequited love.**

For example, if you were Clarice Starling from *The Silence of the Lambs*, you might write: "I was orphaned as a child and placed with an uncle who owned a sheep farm. When the spring lambs were being killed, I tried to save a lamb and failed. I was sent to an orphanage and when I grew up I attended the FBI Academy to protect people from harm. I got my first case. The serial killer I enlisted to help saw that I was atoning for the lamb I couldn't save and agreed to help me. Because of my need to atone, I solve almost every case and am incredibly brave."

E. Atoning:

_____

_____

_____

_____

_____

_____

F. Revenge:

_____

_____

_____

_____

_____

_____

G. Unrequited Love:

_____

_____

_____

_____

_____

_____

Step 1

Creating Your Characters – Exercises

Hero or Heroine

Exercises A – G

Hero or Heroine: Exercise A

A. **Draw your character's family.** Make sure you put your character in the drawing. Select a symbolic object for each member, such as a hat or a baseball bat for a little boy or a bone for a dog. This is not about drawing ability; it is to help you visualize better.

Hero or Heroine: Exercise B

B.   Describe a **formative event** in your character's childhood that could explain why they
do what they do and why they want what they want in your screenplay. For example, if
your character is a cop, you might describe the event that made him or her decide to be
one.

Hero or Heroine: Exercise C

C.   Your characters also have imaginary backgrounds and we must treat them as if they are real people. What were the conflicting "messages" they received from their parents and other influences? How did they reconcile them? For example, how did Michael Corleone reconcile trying to please both himself and his father? Creating this kind of impossible situation is how to get your first draft to be strong.

Hero or Heroine: Exercise D

D. **Define the "spine."** "Spine" is an acting term that is used to mean one of the following: "who the character is," "what the character most wants out of life" and/or the main character's "reason for being." Since the "messages" the character received in the preceding exercise are often contradictory, trying to reconcile them produces the kind of extreme reactions we need for drama. Once you know the character's basic reaction (rebel or please), you will be able to predict how your character will behave in any situation, and this will help you when you plot your screenplay.

Hero or Heroine: Exercises E – G

E.   Write a short paragraph about **atoning** for doing something wrong.

F.   Write a short paragraph describing being wronged and wanting **revenge.**

G.   Write a short paragraph about dealing with **unrequited love.**

Atoning: Frank in *In the Line of Fire:* "I was guarding President Kennedy when he was shot. I couldn't save him. If there had been a few more seconds … I've never forgiven myself. If only I could get a second chance."

E. Atoning:

_____

_____

_____

_____

_____

_____

F. Revenge:

_____

_____

_____

_____

_____

_____

G. Unrequited Love:

_____

_____

_____

_____

_____

_____

Step 1

Creating Your Characters – Exercises

Villain or Obstacle

Exercises A – G

Villain or Obstacle: Exercise A

A. **Draw your character's family.** Make sure you put your character in the drawing. Select a symbolic object for each member, such as a hat or a baseball bat for a little boy or a bone for a dog. This is not about drawing ability; it is to help you visualize better.

Villain or Obstacle: Exercise B

B.   Describe a **formative event** in your character's childhood that could explain why they do what they do and why they want what they want in your screenplay. For example, if your character is a cop, you might describe the event that made him or her decide to be one.

Villain or Obstacle: Exercise C

C.   Your characters also have imaginary backgrounds and we must treat them as if they are real people. What were the conflicting "messages" they received from their parents and other influences? How did they reconcile them? For example, how did Michael Corleone reconcile trying to please both himself and his father? Creating this kind of impossible situation is how to get your first draft to be strong.

Villain or Obstacle: Exercise D

D.   **Define the "spine."**   "Spine" is an acting term that is used to mean one of the following: "who the character is," "what the character most wants out of life" and/or the main character's "reason for being."   Since the "messages" the character received in the preceding exercise are often contradictory, trying to reconcile them produces the kind of extreme reactions we need for drama.   Once you know the character's basic reaction (rebel or please), you will be able to predict how your character will behave in any situation, and this will help you when you plot your screenplay.

Villain or Obstacle: Exercises E – G

E.   Write a short paragraph about **atoning** for doing something wrong.

F.   Write a short paragraph describing being wronged and wanting **revenge.**

G.   Write a short paragraph about dealing with **unrequited love.**

Revenge: Leary in *In the Line of Fire:* "I'm going to kill the President. I've been betrayed by my government. They trained me, turned me into an assassin and now they don't want me anymore. Killing the President seems fair."

E. Atoning:

_____

_____

_____

_____

_____

_____

_____

F. Revenge:

_____

_____

_____

_____

_____

_____

_____

G. Unrequited Love:

_____

_____

_____

_____

_____

_____

_____

Step 1

Creating Your Characters – Exercises

Love Interest

Exercises A – G

*If you do not have a Love Interest character, please skip this section
and go to Sidekick on page 39.*

Love Interest: Exercise A

A. **Draw your character's family.** Make sure you put your character in the drawing. Select a symbolic object for each member, such as a hat or a baseball bat for a little boy or a bone for a dog. This is not about drawing ability; it is to help you visualize better.

Love Interest: Exercise B

B.   Describe a **formative event** in your character's childhood that could explain why they do what they do and why they want what they want in your screenplay. For example, if your character is a cop, you might describe the event that made him or her decide to be one.

Love Interest: Exercise C

C.   Your characters also have imaginary backgrounds and we must treat them as if they are real people. What were the conflicting "messages" they received from their parents and other influences? How did they reconcile them? For example, how did Michael Corleone reconcile trying to please both himself and his father? Creating this kind of impossible situation is how to get your first draft to be strong.

Love Interest: Exercise D

D. **Define the "spine."** "Spine" is an acting term that is used to mean one of the following: "who the character is," "what the character most wants out of life" and/or the main character's "reason for being." Since the "messages" the character received in the preceding exercise are often contradictory, trying to reconcile them produces the kind of extreme reactions we need for drama. Once you know the character's basic reaction (rebel or please), you will be able to predict how your character will behave in any situation, and this will help you when you plot your screenplay.

Love Interest: Exercises E – G

E.   Write a short paragraph about **atoning** for doing something wrong.

F.   Write a short paragraph describing being wronged and wanting **revenge.**

G.   Write a short paragraph about dealing with **unrequited love.**

Unrequited Love: Lily in *In the Line of Fire:* "When I was 15 I was in love with a boy in school, his name was Frank. I never forgot him and swore I would never fall in love with anyone named Frank. You can imagine how I felt when I realized that the creep who thought I was a secretary was named Frank—and I was in love with him, too."

E. Atoning:

_____

_____

_____

_____

_____

_____

F. Revenge:

_____

_____

_____

_____

_____

_____

G. Unrequited Love:

_____

_____

_____

_____

_____

_____

Step 1

Creating Your Characters – Exercises

Sidekick

Exercises A – G

If you do not have a Sidekick character, please skip this section.

Sidekick: Exercise A

A. **Draw your character's family.** Make sure you put your character in the drawing. Select a symbolic object for each member, such as a hat or a baseball bat for a little boy or a bone for a dog. This is not about drawing ability; it is to help you visualize better.

Sidekick: Exercise B

B.   Describe a **formative event** in your character's childhood that could explain why they do what they do and why they want what they want in your screenplay. For example, if your character is a cop, you might describe the event that made him or her decide to be one.

Sidekick: Exercise C

C.   Your characters also have imaginary backgrounds and we must treat them as if they are
real people. What were the conflicting "messages" they received from their parents and
other influences? How did they reconcile them? For example, how did Michael Corleone
reconcile trying to please both himself and his father? Creating this kind of impossible
situation is how to get your first draft to be strong.

Sidekick: Exercise D

D.   **Define the "spine."**   "Spine" is an acting term that is used to mean one of the following: "who the character is," "what the character most wants out of life" and/or the main character's "reason for being." Since the "messages" the character received in the preceding exercise are often contradictory, trying to reconcile them produces the kind of extreme reactions we need for drama. Once you know the character's basic reaction (rebel or please), you will be able to predict how your character will behave in any situation, and this will help you when you plot your screenplay.

Sidekick: Exercises E – G

E.   Write a short paragraph about **atoning** for doing something wrong.

F.   Write a short paragraph describing being wronged and wanting **revenge.**

G.   Write a short paragraph about dealing with **unrequited love.**

Atoning: Al in *In the Line of Fire:* "I let him down that night. If I had gone to investigate the report about Leary, Frank could have stayed out of this."

E. Atoning:

_____

_____

_____

_____

_____

_____

_____

F. Revenge:

_____

_____

_____

_____

_____

_____

_____

G. Unrequited Love:

_____

_____

_____

_____

_____

_____

_____

Step 1

Creating Your Characters – Exercises

Mentor or Other

Exercises A – G

Mentor or Other: Exercise A

A. **Draw your character's family.** Make sure you put your character in the drawing. Select a symbolic object for each member, such as a hat or a baseball bat for a little boy or a bone for a dog. This is not about drawing ability; it is to help you visualize better.

Mentor or Other: Exercise B

B.   Describe a **formative event** in your character's childhood that could explain why they do what they do and why they want what they want in your screenplay. For example, if your character is a cop, you might describe the event that made him or her decide to be one.

Mentor or Other: Exercise C

C. Your characters also have imaginary backgrounds and we must treat them as if they are real people. What were the conflicting "messages" they received from their parents and other influences? How did they reconcile them? For example, how did Michael Corleone reconcile trying to please both himself and his father? Creating this kind of impossible situation is how to get your first draft to be strong.

Mentor or Other: Exercise D

D. **Define the "spine."** "Spine" is an acting term that is used to mean one of the following: "who the character is," "what the character most wants out of life" and/or the main character's "reason for being." Since the "messages" the character received in the preceding exercise are often contradictory, trying to reconcile them produces the kind of extreme reactions we need for drama. Once you know the character's basic reaction (rebel or please), you will be able to predict how your character will behave in any situation, and this will help you when you plot your screenplay.

Mentor or Other: Exercises E – G

E.   Write a short paragraph about **atoning** for doing something wrong.

F.   Write a short paragraph describing being wronged and wanting **revenge.**

G.   Write a short paragraph about dealing with **unrequited love.**

Revenge: Obi-Wan Kenobi in *Star Wars:* "When I received the message from Princess Leia in the droid, my blood boiled and all I wanted to do was risk everything to stop the Empire."

E. Atoning:

_____

_____

_____

_____

_____

_____

F. Revenge:

_____

_____

_____

_____

_____

_____

G. Unrequited Love:

_____

_____

_____

_____

_____

_____

Step 1

Creating Your Characters – Exercises

Blending Plot and Character

Blending Plot and Character Exercise

Now that you've completed your character development, try integrating this information into the story you want to tell by doing the following exercise. This is the first step in pre-visualizing your material.

Try writing out your plot in the three-act structure. Don't worry if you only have a piece—that's a good start.

Start with the end. For example, Clarice Starling catches the killer and saves the intended victim.

Then go back to the beginning and try to place what you have into **three acts.** For example:

Act 1: While still a student at the FBI, Clarice is asked to help on a case. She's eager to help and interviews Hannibal Lector, who gives her a clue.

Act 2: With his help, she is able to overcome many obstacles, and finds the identity of the killer.

Act 3: She confronts the killer, saves his intended victim and atones for the death of the lamb.

The Three-Act Structure

In his seminal book of fragments, *The Poetics*, Aristotle suggested that all stories should have a beginning, a middle and an end. We use Set-Up, Conflict and Resolution as more evocative terms for describing the movements.

Breaking the rhythm of a story into three parts gives us a three-part (act) structure. The word "act" means "the action of carrying something out."

Many screenplays are organized into a three-act structure. The tradition of writing in this form comes from the theater and has been followed by filmmakers. Think of three-act structure as a scaffolding to hold the "house" of your screenplay. Using it will help you build a script that others can easily identify, even if the details are new and original.

Act 1 is the Set-Up. The situation and characters and Conflict are introduced. This is usually around 30 minutes long.

Act 2, which runs approximately 60 minutes, is where the Conflict begins and expands until it reaches a crisis.

In Act 3, the Conflict is resolved, in usually 20-30 minutes.

We will explore this in more detail later when we study the Mythic Journey Map.

This exercise challenges you to do two things: i) take a first crack at writing the end of your story, and ii) insert your characters into your plot using the new knowledge you have about their behaviors.

Remember: Don't get it right—get it written. Set your timer for 15 minutes and give it a try.

Start here. Continue on the following page.

End of Your Story:

_____

_____

_____

_____

_____

_____

Act 1:

Act 2:

Act 3:

STEP 2

PLOT

Answering the Premise-Question

Step 2.   Answering the Premise-Question

We all have something important to say.

A premise, according to the American Heritage Dictionary, is "a proposition upon which an argument is based or from which a conclusion is drawn." I believe we all have an opinion about life or love we want other people to know. However, as Samuel Goldwyn once said, "If you want to send a message, call Western Union." We need to find a way to communicate our point without making a speech. We do this by rephrasing our premise as a question. Your Premise-Question is the backbone of your script. Every word you write should relate back to this central question. The rule of thumb is one Premise-Question per screenplay and every main character must explore and answer the Premise-Question in his/her own way.

The Premise-Question is the motivating power behind everything we do in our own lives. Every decision, every action, every feeling is guided by an opinion we hold about how to best live our life. Every action is an affirmation or rejection of our fundamental convictions. This is also true of your characters.

To make this more concrete, let's look at a very well-written and timeless film, *The Godfather*. The Premise-Question of *The Godfather* can be expressed as: Is family duty more important than living your own life?

The hero, Michael Corleone, believes that the most important thing is self-actualization, but his father becomes unable to manage the "family business" and Michael is forced to make a choice. He is at a crossroads and can only take one path. That's what's at the core of a good dramatic story—both choices relate back to the Premise-Question.

Some additional examples:

1. In *Star Wars,* the Premise-Question is: Does Good conquer Evil? Luke feels powerless and begins by feeling that evil is winning, but by the end of the film the Force teaches him that good always wins against the dark side.

2. In *The Wizard of Oz,* the Premise-Question is: Is free will enough to make you happy? At the beginning, Dorothy feels powerless to save Toto or herself, but by the end she discovers she had the power to go home all along (via the Ruby Slippers) but didn't know enough to

ask. In other words, the Ruby Slippers represented her free will and the journey showed her how to use it.

3. In *In the Line of Fire,* the Premise-Question is: Do you have to resolve the past before you can have a future? At the start of the film, Frank doesn't believe you can resolve the past, and has given up hope. By the end of the film, he has completely changed his mind and is looking forward to the future.

You may find a new Premise-Question that is not on the list. If you do, you can check it by asking if your main character answers the question one way at the beginning and completely changes his or her mind at the end.

Sometimes, no Premise-Question seems quite right. Don't worry; some writers need to write the whole screenplay before the Premise-Question becomes clear. So, if nothing seems to work, then use: Can you please yourself and others? It is foolproof. Simply decide that your hero or heroine answers a firm "yes" or "no" at the beginning and think about how the events of your story push them towards the other answer.

How to Find Your Premise-Question

Study the list of Premise-Questions below, and ask yourself which of the statements best fits your screenplay idea. Then decide what you think your hero or heroine learns in the course of the story. Ask yourself what answer to the Premise-Question would my main character give at the beginning of the story, and what answer would he/she give at the end.

A Few Premise-Questions to Consider:

Premise-Question	Film or Play
Is family duty more important than living your own life?	The Godfather, Moonstruck, In the Mood for Love
Does great love defy even death?	Romeo and Juliet, Titanic, The Fountain, Ghost
Does ruthless ambition lead to its own destruction?	Macbeth, Wall Street, A Few Good Men
Does jealousy destroy itself and the object of its love?	Othello, Misery, She's Gotta Have It
Are the sins of the fathers visited on the children?	Lone Star, Gangs of New York,
Does corporate greed destroy everything in its wake?	Jaws, Poltergeist, Alien, Wall Street, The Lord of War
Is free will enough to make you happy?	The Wizard of Oz, The Matrix, Thelma & Louise, Memento
Does Good conquer Evil?	Star Wars, Spider-Man, High and Low
Can you resolve the past before you can have a future?	In the Line of Fire, The Silence of the Lambs, Eternal Sunshine of the Spotless Mind
Can you please yourself and others?	How to Lose a Guy in 10 Days, Garden State, Tootsie
Can you love without truth?	Rushmore, Vertigo

How to Use the Premise-Question

Write out your Premise-Question by hand and tape it to your computer—where you can see it. As you write, constantly ask yourself if the scene you're working on relates to the Premise-Question.

Write Your Premise-Question Here:

_____

_____

Write your Premise-Question below and cut it out to keep with you when writing.

STEP 3

CHARACTER

Redefining Character in Terms of the Premise-Question

Step 3.   Redefining Character in Terms of the Premise-Question

Now that you've written your Premise-Question, redefining your characters is essential before designing your plot. Ideally, your characters should either affirm or reject your Premise-Question. Usually, however, you need to rework your characters a little bit in order to ensure the necessary crisis of the plot.

The exercises below will help you in three ways:

1.   They will help you visualize your characters in relation to the Premise-Question.

2.   They will give you an overview of the events leading up to your story.

3.   They will give you ideas about how to best organize your plot.

The process outlined by these exercises is similar to the one used in 3-D animation. First you build the bones (Exercise A), then you create behaviors (Exercise B), then you build a story (Exercise C), and, finally, you actually animate your characters (Exercise D).

A.   Three-Dimensional Character Breakdown

Fill out one of these for each major character in your script.

B.   Character / Premise-Question Comparison

Fill this out to determine if your characters serve the Premise-Question that you've defined. Use the information you gleaned from the first exercise. You will do **several of these,** but when you do it for your hero and your villain, ask yourself: Will their opposing points of view lead to a crisis?

If not, you may need to redefine your characters or modify your Premise-Question.

C.   Instant Character-Bio Technique

This powerful technique can be used at any point in your work to generate fresh material, gain insight into your characters, and get an overview of your story.

D.   "You Are What You Eat" Exercise

This visual exercise helps you create an inner life for your characters.

Step 3

Redefining Character in Terms of the Premise-Question

Three-Dimensional Character Breakdown

Three-Dimensional Character Breakdown Exercises

Now that you've decided upon your Premise-Question, redefining your characters in terms of this question is essential before designing your plot, because the Premise-Question is the "spine" of your screenplay. Ideally the "spine" you have chosen for your characters should either affirm or reject your Premise-Question so that your screenplay can arrive at the necessary crisis essential to all drama. For example, if you were writing *The Godfather*, by making sure that Michael Corleone's "spine" is to please his father, it will be easy to choose plot events that put him into conflict with many of the plot events, which will then force him into a series of crises that lead to a climax. This is your goal—to write a screenplay where the character's inner conflict drives the plot. Fill in the chart for the main character as he or she is in the beginning of the film.

For example, if this were Michael Corleone:

Psychological Profile	
Intelligent? Street smart? Innocent? Suspicious?	Intelligent
Personal ambition?	Live life on his own terms
Moral code?	Strong
Attitude towards life?	Optimistic
Temperament?	Laid back
Extrovert? Introvert?	Introvert
Frustrations?	Pleasing self versus father
Romantic/sexual experience?	Lots while he was in the army; faithful to Kay
Emotional problems?	Trying to reconcile his love for his father with the "family business"

Three-Dimensional Character Breakdown – Yourself

1. Write Your Premise-Question: _____
   _____

2. Set the timer for 15 minutes
3. Begin

Physical Description

Sex?

Age?

Height and weight?

Color of hair, eyes, skin?

Posture?

Appearance?

Physical defects?

Cultural Background

Ethnicity? Religion?

Class?

Marital status?

Family history?

Birth order?

How does he/she make money?

Feelings about job?

Education?

Leader or follower?

Political affiliations?

Leisure activities? Friends?

Psychological Profile

Intelligent? Street smart?
Innocent? Suspicious?

Personal ambition?

Moral code?

Attitude towards life?

Temperament?

Extrovert? Introvert?

Frustrations?

Romantic/sexual experience?

Emotional problems?

Obsession?

Inhibitions?

Superstitions?

Phobias?

How does the character feel
about himself/herself?

Three-Dimensional Character Breakdown – Hero or Heroine

1. Write Your Premise-Question: _____

   _____

2. Set the timer for 15 minutes

3. Begin

Physical Description

Sex?

Age?

Height and weight?

Color of hair, eyes, skin?

Posture?

Appearance?

Physical defects?

Cultural Background

Ethnicity? Religion?

Class?

Marital status?

Family history?

Birth order?

How does he/she make money?

Feelings about job?

Education?

Leader or follower?

Political affiliations?

Leisure activities? Friends?

Psychological Profile

Intelligent? Street smart?
Innocent? Suspicious?

Personal ambition?

Moral code?

Attitude towards life?

Temperament?

Extrovert? Introvert?

Frustrations?

Romantic/sexual experience?

Emotional problems?

Obsession?

Inhibitions?

Superstitions?

Phobias?

How does the character feel
about himself/herself?

Three-Dimensional Character Breakdown – Villain or Obstacle

1. Write Your Premise-Question: _____

   _____

2. Set the timer for 15 minutes
3. Begin

Physical Description	
Sex?	
Age?	
Height and weight?	
Color of hair, eyes, skin?	
Posture?	
Appearance?	
Physical defects?	
Cultural Background	
Ethnicity? Religion?	
Class?	
Marital status?	
Family history?	
Birth order?	
How does he/she make money?	
Feelings about job?	
Education?	
Leader or follower?	
Political affiliations?	
Leisure activities? Friends?	

Psychological Profile

Intelligent? Street smart?
Innocent? Suspicious?

Personal ambition?

Moral code?

Attitude towards life?

Temperament?

Extrovert? Introvert?

Frustrations?

Romantic/sexual experience?

Emotional problems?

Obsession?

Inhibitions?

Superstitions?

Phobias?

How does the character feel
about himself/herself?

Three-Dimensional Character Breakdown – Love Interest

1. Write Your Premise-Question: _____
   _____

2. Set the timer for 15 minutes
3. Begin

Physical Description

Sex?

Age?

Height and weight?

Color of hair, eyes, skin?

Posture?

Appearance?

Physical defects?

Cultural Background

Ethnicity? Religion?

Class?

Marital status?

Family history

Birth order?

How does he/she make money?

Feelings about job?

Education

Leader or follower?

Political affiliations?

Leisure activities? Friends?

Psychological Profile

Intelligent? Street smart? Innocent? Suspicious?	
Personal ambition?	
Moral code?	
Attitude towards life	
Temperament	
Extrovert? Introvert?	
Frustrations	
Romantic/sexual experience?	
Emotional problems?	
Obsession?	
Inhibitions?	
Superstitions?	
Phobias?	
How does the character feel about himself/herself?	

Three-Dimensional Character Breakdown – Sidekick

1. Write Your Premise-Question: _____

   _____

2. Set the timer for 15 minutes
3. Begin

Physical Description

Sex?

Age?

Height and weight?

Color of hair, eyes, skin?

Posture?

Appearance?

Physical defects?

Cultural Background

Ethnicity? Religion?

Class?

Marital status?

Family history

Birth order?

How does he/she make money?

Feelings about job?

Education

Leader or follower?

Political affiliations?

Leisure activities? Friends?

Psychological Profile

Intelligent? Street smart?
Innocent? Suspicious?

Personal ambition?

Moral code?

Attitude towards life

Temperament

Extrovert? Introvert?

Frustrations

Romantic/sexual experience?

Emotional problems?

Obsession?

Inhibitions?

Superstitions?

Phobias?

How does the character feel
about himself/herself?

Three-Dimensional Character Breakdown – Mentor or Other

1. Write Your Premise-Question: _____
_____

2. Set the timer for 15 minutes
3. Begin

Physical Description

Sex?

Age?

Height and weight?

Color of hair, eyes, skin?

Posture?

Appearance?

Physical defects?

Cultural Background

Ethnicity? Religion?

Class?

Marital status?

Family history

Birth order?

How does he/she make money?

Feelings about job?

Education

Leader or follower?

Political affiliations?

Leisure activities? Friends?

Psychological Profile	
Intelligent? Street smart? Innocent? Suspicious?	
Personal ambition?	
Moral code?	
Attitude towards life	
Temperament	
Extrovert? Introvert?	
Frustrations	
Romantic/sexual experience?	
Emotional problems?	
Obsession?	
Inhibitions?	
Superstitions?	
Phobias?	
How does the character feel about himself/herself?	

Tip: Whenever writing mentors, remember that they can be bad (The Wizard in *The Wizard of Oz)* or good (Obi-Wan in *Star Wars).*

Step 3

Redefining Character in Terms of the Premise-Question

Character/Premise-Question Comparison

Character/Premise-Question Comparison Exercises

Comparing your characters allows you to see where the key conflicts lie and to make sure that your characters are each having a version of the problem (e.g., family vs. self) suggested by the Premise-Question. If not, you may need to redefine your characters, or modify your Premise-Question. For example, in *In the Line of Fire,* Frank struggles to do something he once failed at—save the President's life. He knows he's being given a chance to resolve his past, but can he use it to create a future?

For example, if your hero and villain were Frank Horrigan and Mitch Leary:

	Frank	**Leary**
Psychological Profile		
Intelligent? Street smart? Innocent? Suspicious?	Intelligent, street smart	Intelligent, suspicious
Personal ambition?	Atoning for past mistakes	Revenge
Moral code?	Moral	Deliberately immoral
Attitude towards life?	Pessimistic	Pessimistic
Temperament?	Ornery SOB	Smooth operator
Extrovert? Introvert?	Introvert	Introvert
Frustrations?	Unable to save President Kennedy or marriage	Cast aside, loyalty spurned
Romantic/sexual experience?	Divorced	Unknown
Emotional problems?	Many (feels powerless)	Many (feels powerless)
Obsession?	Catch Leary; atone for the past by saving current President	Kill the President; see Frank "standing over the grave of another dead President"

Character/Premise-Question Comparison – Villain or Obstacle

1. Write Your Premise-Question: _____

   _____

2. Set the timer for 15 minutes

3. Begin

	Hero or Heroine	Villain or Obstacle
Physical Description		
Sex?		
Age?		
Height and weight?		
Color of hair, eyes, skin?		
Posture?		
Appearance?		
Physical defects?		

Cultural Background

Ethnicity? Religion?

Class?

Marital status?

Family history?

Birth order?

How does he/she make money?

Feelings about job?

Education?

Leader or follower?

Political affiliations?

Leisure activities? Friends?

Psychological Profile

Intelligent? Street smart?
Innocent? Suspicious?

Personal ambition?

Moral code?

Attitude towards life?

Temperament?

Extrovert? Introvert?

Frustrations?

Romantic/sexual experience?

Emotional problems?

Obsession?

Inhibitions?

Superstitions?

Phobias?

How does the character feel about
himself/herself?

Character/Premise-Question Comparison – Love Interest

1. Write Your Premise-Question: _____

   _____

2. Set the timer for 15 minutes

3. Begin

	Hero or Heroine	Love Interest
Physical Description		
Sex?		
Age?		
Height and weight?		
Color of hair, eyes, skin?		
Posture?		
Appearance?		
Physical defects?		

Cultural Background

Ethnicity? Religion?

Class?

Marital status?

Family history?

Birth order?

How does he/she make money?

Feelings about job?

Education?

Leader or follower?

Political affiliations?

Leisure activities? Friends?

Psychological Profile

Intelligent? Street smart?
Innocent? Suspicious?

Personal ambition?

Moral code?

Attitude towards life?

Temperament?

Extrovert? Introvert?

Frustrations?

Romantic/sexual experience?

Emotional problems?

Obsession?

Inhibitions?

Superstitions?

Phobias?

How does the character feel about
himself/herself?

Character/Premise-Question Comparison – Sidekick

1. Write Your Premise-Question: _____

   _____

2. Set the timer for 15 minutes

3. Begin

	Hero or Heroine	Sidekick
Physical Description		
Sex?		
Age?		
Height and weight?		
Color of hair, eyes, skin?		
Posture?		
Appearance?		
Physical defects?		

Cultural Background

Ethnicity? Religion?

Class?

Marital status?

Family history?

Birth order?

How does he/she make money?

Feelings about job?

Education?

Leader or follower?

Political affiliations?

Leisure activities? Friends?

Psychological Profile

Intelligent? Street smart?
Innocent? Suspicious?

Personal ambition?

Moral code?

Attitude towards life?

Temperament?

Extrovert? Introvert?

Frustrations?

Romantic/sexual experience?

Emotional problems?

Obsession?

Inhibitions?

Superstitions?

Phobias?

How does the character feel about
himself/herself?

Character/Premise-Question Comparison – Mentor or Other

1. Write Your Premise-Question: _____
   _____

2. Set the timer for 15 minutes
3. Begin

	Hero or Heroine	Mentor or Other
Physical Description		
Sex?		
Age?		
Height and weight?		
Color of hair, eyes, skin?		
Posture?		
Appearance?		
Physical defects?		

Cultural Background

Ethnicity? Religion?

Class?

Marital status?

Family history?

Birth order?

How does he/she make money?

Feelings about job?

Education?

Leader or follower?

Political affiliations?

Leisure activities? Friends?

Psychological Profile

Intelligent? Street smart?
Innocent? Suspicious?

Personal ambition?

Moral code?

Attitude towards life?

Temperament?

Extrovert? Introvert?

Frustrations?

Romantic/sexual experience?

Emotional problems?

Obsession?

Inhibitions?

Superstitions?

Phobias?

How does the character feel about
himself/herself?

Step 3

Redefining Character in Terms of the Premise-Question

Instant Character-Bio Technique

Instant Character-Bio Technique

Clustering is an efficient alternative to the traditional character biography. It not only gives you insight, it helps you generate images, scenes and bits of dialogue that add up to a main character's life in a more intuitive, less fact-oriented way. After you cluster, you will find that writing as if you are the character will give you a great deal of information with very little effort.

1.   Start by placing your character's name in the center. Remember to start with yourself.

2.   Circle it.

3.   Using a timer, take 3-5 minutes to free-associate as many things about your character as you can think of.

4.   Write and circle these things as they come to you. Connect the circles back to your character however you see fit.

5.   After a few minutes, you will feel an urge to write. Pick whichever word appeals to you the most. Set the timer for 5 minutes and write in the first person, present tense. For example, "My father died when I was a little girl. All I ever wanted to do was please him and catch those bad guys who got away."

There is no wrong way of doing this! Have fun!

Sample cluster from *The Silence of the Lambs*

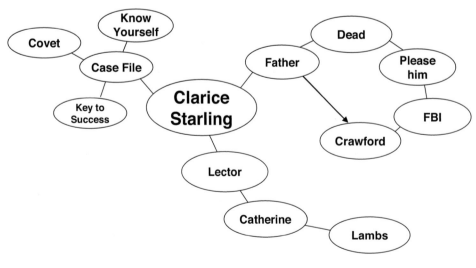

Instant Character-Bio Technique – Yourself

Expand this cluster:

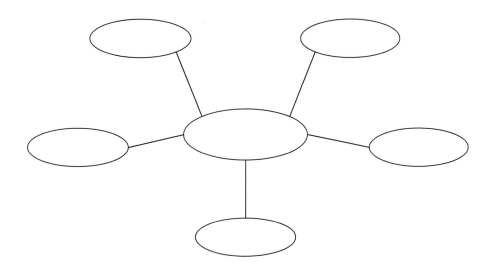

Write here:

_____

_____

_____

_____

_____

_____

Instant Character-Bio Technique – Hero or Heroine

Expand this cluster:

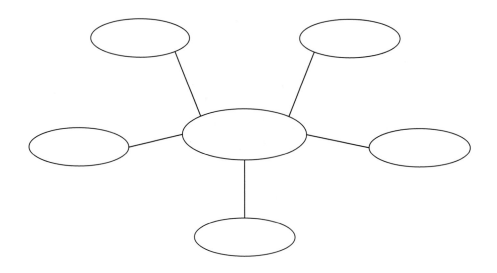

Write here:

_____

_____

_____

_____

_____

_____

Instant Character-Bio Technique – Villain or Obstacle

Expand this cluster:

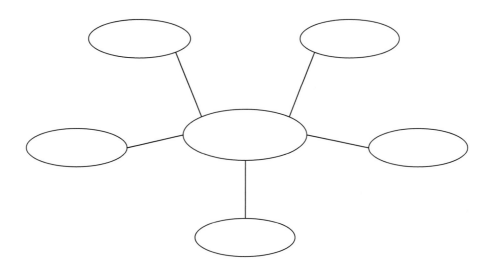

Write here:

_____

_____

_____

_____

_____

_____

Instant Character-Bio Technique – Love Interest

Expand this cluster:

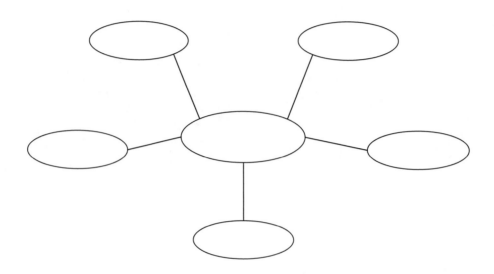

Write here:

_____

_____

_____

_____

_____

_____

Instant Character-Bio Technique – Sidekick

Expand this cluster:

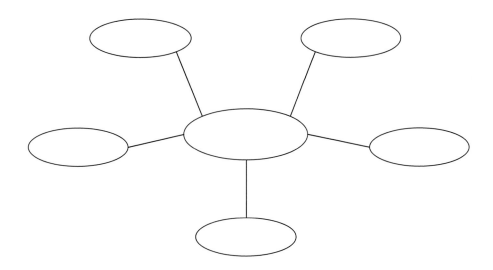

Write here:

_____

_____

_____

_____

_____

_____

Instant Character-Bio Technique – Mentor or Other

Expand this cluster:

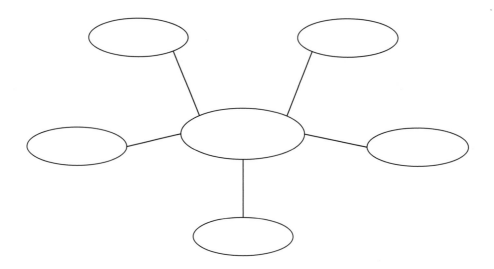

Write here:

_____

_____

_____

_____

_____

Step 3

Redefining Character in Terms of the Premise-Question

The "You Are What You Eat" Technique

The "You Are What You Eat" Technique

One of the most fun things to write about is food. And like real people, your characters are what they eat. When we eat food, we remember other experiences of eating it. In real life the process is called remembering. In writing, it's called "making it up." One of the basic principles that I teach is that it is much easier to remember things than to make them up. The purpose of this exercise is to create memories for your character that don't exist, creating the illusion that you are "remembering" your character's experience.

Pick **one** of the following choices: **i) Favorite food, ii) Most hated food** or **iii) Comfort food** for yourself, your Hero or Heroine, and other main characters. Work quickly, and don't try to "effort" it. Set your timer for 15 minutes and complete the following three-part exercise:

First, decide which food experience you want you or your character to "remember." In the middle circle of the top cluster on the next page write "favorite," "hated" or "comfort." Free-associate images or ideas relating to your food choice.

Next, pick the most appealing item from this first cluster. In the middle circle of the bottom cluster on the next page write this new choice. Free-associate a time when you (or your character) "ate" this favorite, most hated or comfort food around this new circle. You will feel a strong desire to write after 2-3 minutes.

Finally, write for a paragraph or so, describing the food and telling a story about the circumstances surrounding the eating of the food. You will be amazed at what you can learn. Often, the best scenes in a screenplay come out of the exercise.

For example, if your character were Vincent Vega in *Pulp Fiction*, talking about his favorite food:

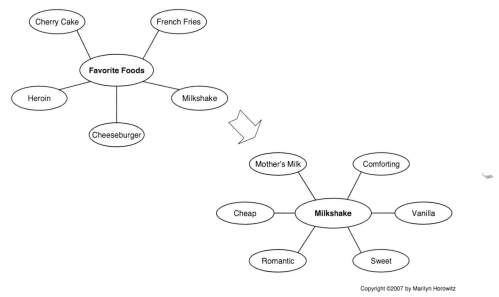

Copyright ©2007 by Marilyn Horowitz

Favorite Food Story

My boss, Marcellus, asked me to baby-sit his wife while he was away on business. She wanted to go to a retro 50s joint; I was very nervous, but she insisted on ordering a vanilla milkshake, my favorite. I couldn't believe it cost five dollars, but when it came it was worth every penny. Oh, and later we won the dance contest.

"You Are What You Eat" Technique – Yourself

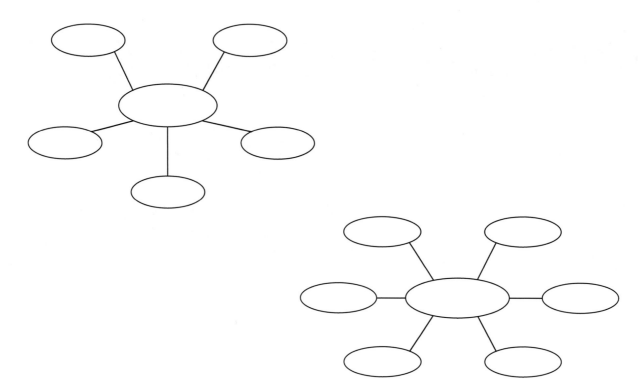

Yourself:

_____

_____

_____

_____

_____

_____

"You Are What You Eat" Technique – Hero or Heroine

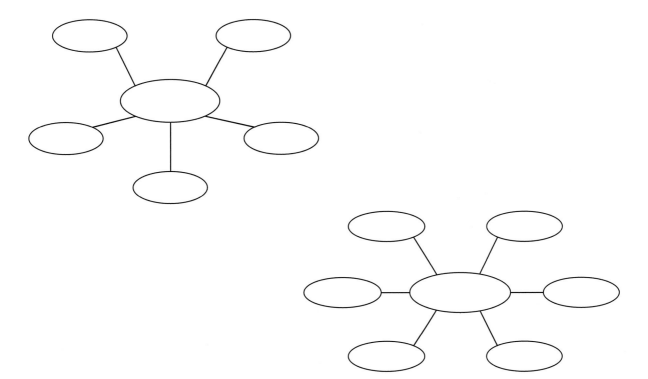

Hero or Heroine:

_____

_____

_____

_____

_____

_____

"You Are What You Eat" Technique – Villain or Obstacle

Villain or Obstacle:

_____

_____

_____

_____

_____

_____

"You Are What You Eat" Technique – Love Interest

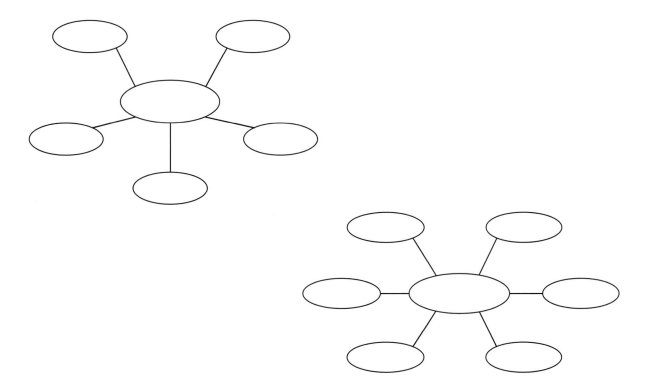

Love Interest:

_____

_____

_____

_____

_____

_____

"You Are What You Eat" Technique – Sidekick

Sidekick:

_____

_____

_____

_____

_____

_____

_____

"You Are What You Eat" Technique – Mentor or Other

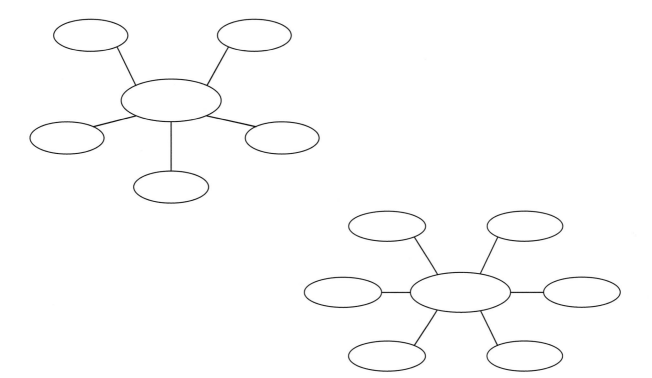

Mentor or Other:

_____

_____

_____

_____

_____

_____

STEP 4

PLOT

Plot Your Screenplay

Step 4

Plot Your Screenplay

Part I.

The Mythic Journey Map and

the Three Levels of Conflict

The Mythic Journey Map

1 Ordinary World (Set-Up)

2 Call to Adventure (Conflict)

3 Refusal of the Call (Resolution)

4 Meeting w/ Helper/Mentor (Set-Up)

5 Crossing the First Threshold (Conflict)

6 Tests, Helpers, Enemies (Resolution)

7 Approach to the Innermost Cave (Set-Up)

8 Ordeal & Flight (Conflict)

9 Reward (Resolution)

10 The Road Back (Set-Up)

11 Resurrection (Conflict)

12 Return with the Elixir (Resolution)

ACT I (Set-Up)

ACT II, Part 1 (Conflict)

ACT II, Part 2

ACT III (Resolution)

What is the world of the story?

What happens to get the story started?

How does the main character deny the need for change?

Does the main character meet a mentor?

Does the main character enter a new world?

Who/what are the new friends and obstacles our main character meets?

How do the stakes go up? How does this send the main character in a new direction?

How do things get bad enough to create a crisis?

How does this crisis cause the main character to change?

What is the preparation for the final climax?

How does the main character change?

What is the final showdown? Does Everyone live happily ever after or not?

Caveat emptor: As Joseph Campbell says in *Hero with a Thousand Faces* (p. 246), "Many tales isolate and greatly enlarge upon one or two of the typical elements of the full cycle ... others string a number of independent cycles into a single series ... differing characters or episodes can become fused or a single episode can reduplicate itself and reappear under many changes."

Part 1:   Plot Your Screenplay Using the Mythic Journey Map

The Mythic Journey Map provides a flexible structure that allows you to tell your story the way you want to but keeps it in a commercially presentable form. Think of the Map as the wine bottle you will pour the new "wine" of your story line into.

First, let's define Plot as the events that make up your screenplay. Your job as a screenwriter is not only to make up the story, but also to decide the best way to tell it.

What Joseph Campbell wrote about in his book *The Hero with a Thousand Faces* was that all great mythic stories, such as *The Odyssey* and *Gone with the Wind*, have a basic universal story. This story involves a hero or heroine who takes a journey which leads him or her to some kind of self-realization through struggle. The flow of this journey is so pleasing that emulating it almost always ensures a rewarding experience for both storyteller and audience.

What I've discovered is that this journey is actually two voyages along the same highway: an **Action Journey,** which happens throughout the plot, and an **Emotional Journey,** which follows the character's feelings about what is happening to them and parallels the Action Journey. The Action Journey is the plot, and the Emotional Journey is how the hero or heroine responds to the plot and gains new insights, which cause him or her to succeed in their quest. Or not.

The Mythic Journey Map: Action Journey

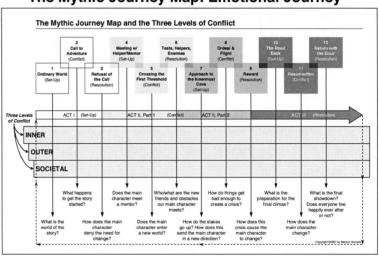

(See page 115)

The Mythic Journey Map: Emotional Journey

(See page 124)

The key is to organize the plot and then identify your main character's conflicts. This is why you have done all of the character work in earlier chapters, so that you are well-prepared for the steps that follow. A screenplay built this way always tells a story that your audience can connect with, whether it's drama, like *Casablanca,* or science fiction, like *Star Wars*.

Part 1: The Mythic Journey Map

When I began in this business, I sold a novel and was asked to adapt it and write the screenplay. I had a terrible time, and finally, in a dream, Joseph Campbell appeared to me, dressed in a toga, sitting in a tree. I asked him for help and complained that his stuff was too complicated and abstract for me. He asked, "What do you need to finish your script?" I thought about it, and even though I was asleep, I knew this was a pivotal moment in my life. If I didn't ask for the right thing, I would fail. I thought and thought, and finally said, "I need a map." He nodded. "If I give you one, will you use it?" I reminded him that I was a New Yorker and it would depend. He laughed and I woke up and, still half-asleep, drew a rough version of the Mythic Journey Map. As a result of my dream, I was able to use the Map and finish my script with ease.

Marilyn's Dream Map

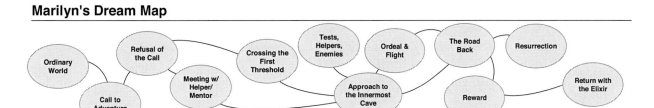

Copyright ©2007 by Marilyn Horowitz

When setting up this map, I had to not only create it, but also to define the ground it would cover. Since many movies are two hours long, especially classic movies, the basis of the map is a hypothetical 120-minute film.

When we think about drama we naturally divide stories into three parts, as Aristotle suggested: a beginning, a middle and an end. We refer to these parts as **Set-Up, Conflict** and **Resolution**. There are 12 sequences in the Mythic Journey Map, and therefore four repetitions of this basic three-part dramatic structure in each film.

The Mythic Journey Map

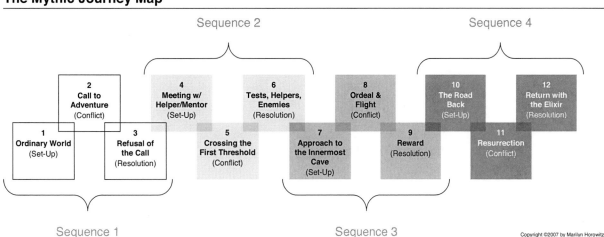

Copyright ©2007 by Marilyn Horowitz

The traditional three-act structure has been adjusted to reflect this. Act 2 has been separated into Act 2, Part 1, and Act 2, Part 2.

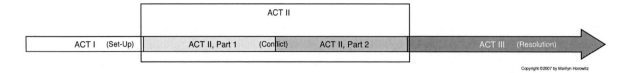

The statements in the boxes at the top of the Map are how I refer to each of the 12 sequences. For example, the opening sequence will be referred to as the "Ordinary World." The second one will be referred to as the "Call to Adventure," and so on for all 12 sequences throughout the book.

Each of the 12 sequences asks a question that must be answered in the allotted section. Treat each sequence as a mini movie that has its own Set-Up, Conflict and Resolution.

The Mythic Journey Map

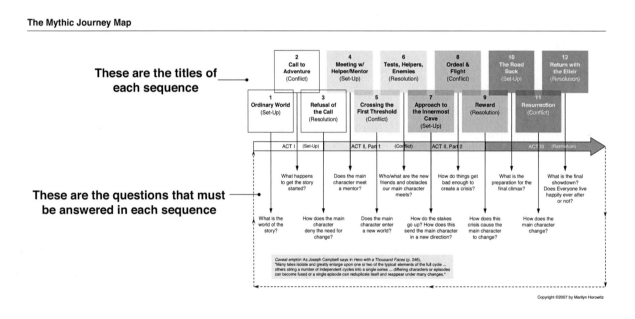

The best way to understand the Map is to deconstruct films. In the analysis that follows we will look at three films. I selected these films because they are simple and easy to follow, and have both enjoyed lasting commercial success. *Star Wars* follows a hero's journey and *The Wizard of Oz* is a heroine's journey. *In the Line of Fire* is a contemporary film which has a well-defined villain.

The principle behind this exercise is that we learn best by watching others. By watching these three masterpieces it will shorten your apprenticeship and take you quickly to mastery of screenplay form.

Analysis of the 12 Sequences

Remember: **Getting the audience to sympathize with your hero or heroine is the most important task of the screenwriter.**

1.   The Ordinary World (What is the world of the story?)

This sequence introduces the main characters and their situations before anything changes. Think of it as covering the "5 W's" you learned in school: who, what, when, where and why.

In *Star Wars*, Darth Vader captures Princess Leia's ship. She plants the message for Obi-Wan in R2-D2, who escapes with C-3PO. This message is what lets us know that Obi-Wan must be found or all is lost.

In *The Wizard of Oz*, we meet Dorothy, Toto, Miss Gulch, Auntie Em and the farmhands. In the first scene, we learn that Toto has dug up Miss Gulch's flowerbed <u>again</u>. It's this key fact, that Toto has <u>done it before</u>, that lets us know that we are coming in just before a moment of crisis. This lets the audience know why the story is beginning at this particular moment in time.

In *In the Line of Fire*, Frank and his partner, Al, capture a pair of counterfeiters. Al is almost killed, but later Frank talks him out of quitting. Frank checks out a report that someone is planning to kill the President. When Frank checks the report, he discovers that the would-be assassin has created a shrine of hate and may pose a legitimate threat. Frank brushes off his concern and tells the landlady that the Secret Service receives 1,400 such reports per year and there's no need to worry. Meanwhile, the would-be assassin, Mitch Leary, a former CIA agent, has been out grocery shopping and "just happens" to look up at his window in time to both realize he's been busted and to recognize Frank. This is the one coincidence in the film. If Frank had done his job and reported the threat, Leary would not have seen him and there would be no story. A good rule of thumb is no more than one coincidence per film—unless it's a comedy, in which case you're allowed two.

2.   The Call to Adventure (What happens to get the story started?)

This is where something has to happen that forces our hero or heroine to act. This sequence is pretty straightforward.

In *Star Wars*, Luke sees the hidden message from Princess Leia inside R2-D2, and in *The Wizard of Oz*, Toto escapes from Miss Gulch. In *In the Line of Fire*, Frank finds evidence of a plan to kill the President.

3.   The Refusal of the Call (How does the main character deny the need for change?)

This is the most critical and most difficult sequence to plot. The hero or heroine resists the very thing he or she wants. The goal of this sequence is to force the hero or heroine to make an impossible choice.

When Obi-Wan asks Luke if he wants to become a Jedi Knight, Luke of course wants to, but has to refuse because of his loyalty to his aunt and uncle. And in films, like real life, the stakes are always about what you want to do and what you feel you have to do. Think of any holiday when you are asked to do different things by the different people you love. You find yourself on the horns of a dilemma because you literally can't be in two places at once, and so it should be with the characters in screenplays.

In *The Wizard of Oz*, Dorothy can't run away to save Toto while at the same time go home to her aunt. She chooses her aunt over Toto out of guilt as much as love, as we, ourselves, often do.

In *In the Line of Fire*, Frank almost has a heart attack as he runs alongside the presidential limo. He can't heed the call because of his health. He is also unable to persuade the Chief of Staff to call off an upcoming dinner. There's one more thing that must be done in this sequence. You must add an event that takes the story in a different direction—towards the arena of Act 2.

For example, in *Star Wars*, Luke sees part of Princess Leia's message; in *The Wizard of Oz*, there's a tornado; and in *In the Line of Fire*, Leary sends Frank on a wild goose chase to the wrong house.

4.   Meeting with the Mentor (Does the main character meet a mentor?)

The hero or heroine meets someone who sends them in a new direction, for better or worse.

In *Star* Wars, Luke is saved by Obi-Wan and learns about the Force. In *The Wizard of Oz*, Dorothy meets Glinda, the Good Witch. In *In the Line of Fire*, Frank gets a call from Leary at the office. This is an unusual case because the villain is acting as the mentor.

5.   Crossing the First Threshold (Does the main character enter a new world?)

The main character literally or figuratively changes location.

Luke is saved from the Sand People by Obi-Wan and learns about his father, Dorothy lands in Oz, and Frank goes from D.C. to Denver.

6. **Test, Helpers, Enemies** (Who/what are the new friends and obstacles our main character meets?)

In this new world, the hero or heroine must navigate through unfamiliar terrain and find his or her place in the new world.

Stormtroopers destroy Luke's home. Dorothy must take the Yellow Brick Road. Frank mistakenly thinks he hears gunshots, embarrasses the President and gets thrown off the team.

7. **Approach to the Innermost Cave** (How do the stakes go up? How does this send the main character in a new direction?)

A new event or goal presents itself and must be overcome before the main character can attain the goal.

The *Millennium Falcon* gets trapped in the Death Star. Dorothy and her friends must get to the castle. Frank and Al get a solid lead to Leary.

8. **Ordeal and Flight** (How do things get bad enough to create a crisis?)

An unexpected crisis occurs that very nearly causes failure.

Luke and the others are trapped in the trash compactor. Dorothy is trapped in the Witch's castle. Frank and Al are almost shot by the CIA at Leary's home.

9. **Reward** (How does the crisis cause the main character to change?)

The main character learns information that takes him or her in a new direction so he or she can win the battle in Act 3. Obi-Wan fights Vader and dies, so Luke must carry on without him. Dorothy returns to Oz only to learn that Oz is a fraud and has no power. Frank chases Leary, who saves him, but kills Al.

10. **The Road Back** (What is the preparation for the final climax?)

The hero or heroine prepares for the Climax.

The Rebels prepare to attack the Death Star.

The Wizard offers to get Dorothy home via hot-air balloon.

Frank and Leary each prepare for the presidential dinner.

11. Resurrection (How does the main character change?)

The main character's new behavior is not enough to overcome the final obstacle, and he or she must accept greater responsibility for the outcome.

As the attack on the Death Star turns toward a disaster, Luke hears Obi-Wan telling him to use the Force, and he does. Glinda appears and tells Dorothy the Ruby Slippers give her the power to return home at any time, and that all she has to do is to click her heels together. Frank figures out the anagram and closes in on Leary.

12. Return with the Elixir (What is the final showdown? Does everyone live happily ever after or not?)

The main character overcomes the final obstacle to attaining his or her goal—or not.

Luke fires the critical shot and the Death Star is blown up. Dorothy clicks her heels together and returns to Kansas. Frank saves the President and faces off with Leary. And they all live happily ever after.

How the Map Works

Each of the 12 sequences covers roughly 10 minutes of screen time. On a regular map you would use latitude and longitude to determine where you are in order to chart a course to your destination. The Mythic Journey Map uses **where you are** on the Map (e.g., the Ordinary World) and the **sequence question** (e.g., what is the World of the Story?) as the two points of navigation.

A scene is the basic currency of drama. Adam Nadler, an esteemed colleague, tells his students to think of each scene as having three mini-acts. Borrowing this wonderful idea, we will define a scene as a mini-film that has a beginning, middle and end, and that advances the plot and reveals character. A scene can vary in length, but a rule of thumb is to use a ratio of 1-2-1 to decide how much of each part you need. The set-up and resolution should be roughly half the length of the conflict portion. Another rule of thumb is to aim for three pages, or three minutes, for a scene.

We translate this information directly into our writing because screenplay format is designed so that one page equals one minute of screen time. Each 10-minute/page sequence is comprised of a series of scenes that answer the question asked in that particular sequence, which addresses the Action Journey.

The Mythic Journey Map and the Three Levels of Conflict

Act	#	Stage	INNER	OUTER	SOCIETAL
ACT I (Set-Up)	1	Ordinary World (Set-Up)	What is the world of the story?		
	2	Call to Adventure (Conflict)	How does the main character deny the need for change?	What happens to get the story started?	
	3	Refusal of the Call (Resolution)	Does the main character meet a mentor?	How does the main character deny the need for change?	
ACT II, Part 1 (Set-Up / Conflict)	4	Meeting w/ Helper/Mentor (Set-Up)	Does the main character enter a new world?	Does the main character meet a mentor?	
	5	Crossing the First Threshold (Conflict)	Who/what are the new friends and obstacles our main character meets?	Does the main character enter a new world?	
	6	Tests, Helpers, Enemies (Resolution)	How do the stakes go up? How does this send the main character in a new direction?	Who/what are the new friends and obstacles our main character meets?	
ACT II, Part 2 (Conflict)	7	Approach to the Innermost Cave (Set-Up)	How do things get bad enough to create a crisis?	How do the stakes go up? How does this send the main character in a new direction?	
	8	Ordeal & Flight (Conflict)	How does this crisis cause the main character to change?	How do things get bad enough to create a crisis?	
	9	Reward (Resolution)	What is the preparation for the final climax?	How does this crisis cause the main character to change?	
ACT III (Resolution)	10	The Road Back (Set-Up)	How does the main character change?	What is the preparation for the final climax?	
	11	Resurrection (Conflict)	What is the final showdown? Does everyone live happily ever after or not?	How does the main character change?	
	12	Return with the Elixir (Resolution)		What is the final showdown? Does everyone live happily ever after or not?	

Three Levels of Conflict

INNER
OUTER
SOCIETAL

The Three Levels of Conflict

As you saw when you did the character exercises, your creations are as rich as any real-life person. Now the trick is to keep the essence of this complexity and use it in your screenplay, and to create the maximum conflict for your hero or heroine.

When plotting, the scene-selection process needs to be made systematic because writers always want to tell more story that can fit into a film.

There is often a lot of chaos at the beginning, but it can be avoided by using these processes. Asking the three questions as we work allows us to thread the Three Levels of Conflict through the Mythic Journey Map, entwining them into a single DNA strand, focusing consistently on plot, subplot and inner conflict. Each scene will start off well-structured with good dialogue, and most importantly the subtext, often the hardest part, will already be there.

What is Subtext?

According to Constantin Stanislavski, the great acting teacher, subtext is the deeper and usually repressed meanings of your hero or heroine's dialogue and actions. It is what a character really feels, whether or not it matches what he or she is saying or doing.

Here are a few examples of subtext:

1. In the wedding scene in *The Godfather*, Vito refuses to take the wedding picture unless Michael will pose with the family. Michael agrees, and then gestures for Kay to join them. That is the action or the "text" of the scene. The subtext reflects the Premise-Question. Michael is being asked to "join" the family, and although he doesn't realize it consciously, when he invites Kay into the picture, he has made the choice to follow his family duty, not his own life.

2. In *Star Wars*, when Luke battles Darth Vader, the text or action is good versus evil, but the subtext is the battle between a father and son who are on opposite sides.

3. In *The Wizard of Oz*, the action of the story is about a powerless Dorothy trying to get home, but the subtext is about free will and perception—she felt helpless, but she really had the power via the Ruby Slippers to go home all along.

4. In *In the Line of Fire*, when Frank offers to check out the threat against the President so that Al can go home to his family, it seems like a considerate thing to do, but the subtext is

that Frank feels guilty for almost getting Al killed. He assumes guilt because he always feels that he is in the wrong.

Subtext creates conflict, and vice versa. Conflict is the juice that makes a screenplay powerful and marketable.

What is Conflict?

Conflict is what happens when your hero or heroine is blocked from getting what he or she wants at any point in your script. By choosing the areas of a character's life where there is the most conflict, you will force your characters to struggle harder to get what they want, which creates better drama.

What ruins most screenplays is that there is not enough conflict because the stakes for the hero or heroine are not high enough. The stakes must be life or death. In a comedy or drama, the definition of "death" is a metaphor. In *Tootsie*, Michael is willing to become a woman to become a star, "killing off" his male self. In *Witness*, John Book gives up being in love to capture the bad guys. He is willing to let the part of him that is in love "die."

In the films we are studying, death is not a metaphor. In *Star Wars*, Luke accepts certain death to save the Resistance because it's the right thing to do and to honor his lost father. *In The Wizard of Oz*, Dorothy risks death to get the Witch's broom so she can go home, because she is an orphan and has lost her home once before. In *In the Line of Fire*, Frank faces death to save a President because he once failed to do so.

When plotting, keep in mind that men and women generally have work, family and love as the focal points of their lives, while children have family, school and friends. Finding the areas where the character is having the most trouble succeeding will help you plot your screenplay.

How the Three Levels of Conflict Works

In order to apply the Three Levels of Conflict to your screenplay, you must consider the Premise-Question first. As you remember, when we studied the Premise-Question, this is the backbone of any film. Everything connects back to this core question as well as being shaped by it. As you're trying to identify the Three Levels of Conflict, keep the Premise-Question in mind.

Every scene, every line, every choice must relate back to the Premise-Question.

The Premise-Question for *In the Line of Fire* is: Do you have to resolve the past before you can have a future?

Now, holding your Premise-Question in mind, we will now use the technique, which is asking these three questions:

1. "What is my main character's inner conflict?"

Inner conflict is what drives a hero or heroine's actions even though we can't see it on-screen. Inner conflict is what is inside the character that holds him or her back. For example, in *In the Line of Fire* Frank feels he is a failure in both work and love. He feels doomed by his past, which is the challenge he must overcome. The Premise-Question should always reflect the hero's inner conflict.

In Act 1, Frank goes to examine Leary's room and the threat to kill the President; he decides not to report it. This scene dramatizes his inner conflict, his inner feeling of powerlessness.

In the middle of Act 2, Frank is at the Chicago rally and has the flu. He has to decide whether or not to follow his hunch that Leary will make an attempt on the President's life. Frank thinks the flashbulbs going off are bullets and creates a scene. This embarrasses the President and gets Frank fired from the team. The scene also dramatizes his inner conflict, and shows us how he has changed; he has begun to believe in himself again.

2. "What is his/her outer conflict?"

What is preventing your main character from succeeding? Leary comes into the picture and forces Frank to prove he can save another President. Lily, the love interest, also forces him to try to overcome his past failure in love. The outer conflict is the plot of the story: Frank's quest to stop Leary and the subplot with Lily. Can you identify these elements for your screenplay?

3. "What is the societal conflict?"

This level of conflict takes place on-screen on a larger playing field than the outer conflict, and is often both the world of the story and what thematically links the three levels together. The world of the Secret Service, which protects our President, is where the societal conflict of *In the Line of Fire* takes place. A societal theme is that Leary and Frank are both civil servants who have failed. Leary has sworn revenge while Frank has accepted his fate.

Putting It All Together

As mentioned previously, experience is the best way to learn. It's been said that experience is what's left after you've forgotten what you've learned. The System's intention is that you suffer through this steep learning curve over the course of a few films before it becomes second nature. What I discovered that is truly exciting is that we organize our real-life experience in a similar way to the three-act structure, so really we've already had a lot of practice.

Watch these three films, *Star Wars, The Wizard of Oz* and *In the Line of Fire,* in 10-minute chunks, periodically stopping the film and comparing what you have just watched with the Film Deconstruction Chart that has been filled in for each of these films at the end of this section.

You should watch the films **before** you study the Deconstruction Charts, because it's critical that you learn to pre-visualize your own screenplay, as if it <u>were already a finished film,</u> **before** you try to put it into words. If you can **see** it, you can **write** it.

As we look at the Mythic Map for *Star Wars, The Wizard of Oz,* and *In the Line of Fire*, you will notice there is both rigidity and flexibility in this mythic structure. Holding paradox is the key to originality. Rather than to think in terms of either/or, try to think in terms of and/also. Not either rigid or flexible, but rather rigid and also flexible.

Step 4

Plot Your Screenplay

Part II.

Film Deconstruction

Step 4

Plot Your Screenplay

A. Deconstruction of
Star Wars and *The Wizard of Oz*

Deconstruction of *Star Wars* and *The Wizard of Oz*

Watch *Star Wars* and *The Wizard of Oz* as you consult the completed Film Deconstruction Charts. After each 10-minute chunk, stop the film and look at the list of scenes, and consider if they answer the question asked at that point in the Mythic Journey Map, and if the Three Levels of Conflict are addressed.

Film Deconstruction Chart – *Star Wars*

Page / Sequence	10 min / "Ordinary World" What is the world of the story?	20 min / "Call to Adventure" What happens to get the story started?	30 min / "Refusal of the Call" How does the main character deny the need for change?
		ACT I	
Plot	Diplomatic Ship: Leia cannot escape the Empire, leaves message in R2-D2 (5:00) Vader attacks in search of Death Star plans and passengers (6:11) R2-D2 escapes with C-3PO with message for help (7:00)	Tatooine: Jawas capture R2-D2 and C-3PO (12:00) Stormtroopers search for plans from the escape pod (15:15) Jawas sell R2-D2 and C-3PO to Luke and his uncle (17:30)	Luke sees part of Leia's message intended for Obi-Wan (21:00) Luke learns Obi-Wan died with his father (24:30) Uncle Owen tells Luke he can't leave the farm early for the academy (25:00)
On-screen Relationships (Outer Conflict)	Leia & R2-D2 R2-D2 & C-3PO Leia & Vader	R2-D2 & C-3PO R2-D2, C-3PO & Jawas Luke & R2-D2, C-3PO	Luke & R2-D2, C-3PO Luke & Uncle, Aunt
Hero or Heroine's Needs (Inner Conflict)	Leia: Get message left in R2-D2 to help	Luke: Learn about the rebellion against the Empire	Luke: Get Uncle's permission to submit application to the academy, leave the farm
Villain's Needs (Societal Conflict)	Vader's need: Capture Leia, retrieve Death Star plans and discover location of the Rebel base.	Retrieve Death Star plans and discover location of the Rebel base	Retrieve Death Star plans and discover location of the Rebel base

Film Deconstruction Chart – *Star Wars*

	40 min / "Meeting w/ Helper/Mentor" Does the main character meet a mentor?	ACT II – Part 1 50 min / "Crossing the First Threshold" Does the main character enter a new world?	60 min / "Tests, Helpers, Enemies" Who/what are the new friends and obstacles our main character meets?
Page / Sequence			
Plot	R2-D2 escapes to find Obi-Wan (27:00) Obi-Wan saves Luke from Sand People (30:00) Obi-Wan explains Jedi and Empire history, gives Luke his father's lightsaber, explains the Force (33:00)	Stormtroopers destroy Luke's home (40:12) Vader tortures Leia (41:37) Luke chooses to join Obi-Wan (42:27)	Luke and Obi-Wan meet Han Solo in search for a fast ship (48:00) Han gets more time to pay back Jabba the Hut (53:00) The *Millennium Falcon* escapes the Empire (56:46) Vader destroys Alderon (59:00)
On-screen Relationships (Outer Conflict)	Luke & R2-D2, C-3PO Luke & Obi-Wan	Luke & Obi-Wan Leia & Vader	Luke, Obi-Wan & Han Han & Jabba Leia & Vader
Hero or Heroine's Needs (Inner Conflict)	Luke: Find R2-D2, decide to help Obi-Wan get to Alderon Leia: Instruct Obi-Wan to get R2-D2 to Alderon via message	Luke: Travel to Alderon, find a pilot at Mos Eisley Leia: Protect the location of the Rebel base	Luke: Travel to Alderon Leia: Protect the location of the Rebel base
Villain's Needs (Societal Conflict)	Retrieve Death Star plans and discover location of the Rebel base	Retrieve Death Star plans and discover location of the Rebel base	Retrieve Death Star plans and discover location of the Rebel base

Film Deconstruction Chart – *Star Wars*

ACT II – Part 2

Page / Sequence	70 min / **"Approach to Innermost Cave"** How do the stakes go up? How does this send the main character in a new direction?	80 min / **"Ordeal & Flight"** How do things get bad enough to create a crisis?	90 min / **"Reward"** How does the crisis cause the main character to change?
Plot	Luke learns the Force (60:45) *Millennium Falcon* is trapped in the Death Star (65:13) Luke and Han disguise themselves as Stormtroopers to free the *Millennium Falcon* from the Death Star (68:41)	R2-D2 finds Leia onboard the Death Star (70:47) Luke convinces Han to fight their way into the cell block to save Leia (75:00) Luke and Leia meet (76:00) Vader sense Obi-Wan's presence (77:00)	Luke, Leia, and Han are trapped in the garbage compactor (79:00) R2-D2 saves the group (84:00) Obi-Wan shuts down the grid (86:00) Obi-Wan and Vader meet (90:17) Vader kills Obi-Wan (92:25)
On-screen Relationships (Outer Conflict)	Luke & Obi-Wan Luke, Obi-Wan & Han	Luke, Obi-Wan & Han Luke & Han Luke & Leia	Luke, Leia & Han R2-D2 & C-3PO Obi-Wan & Vader
Hero or Heroine's Needs (Inner Conflict)	Luke: Escape from the Death Star	Luke: Save Leia, escape from the Death Star	Luke: Get Leia to Obi-Wan, escape from the Death Star
Villain's Needs (Societal Conflict)	Retrieve Death Star plans and destroy the Rebel base	Kill Obi-Wan, retrieve Death Star plans and destroy the Rebel base`	Kill Obi-Wan, retrieve Death Star plans and destroy the Rebel base

Film Deconstruction Chart – *Star Wars*

	ACT III		
Page / Sequence	**100 min / "The Road Back"** What is the preparation for the final climax?	**110 min / "Resurrection"** How does the main character change?	**120 min / "Return w/ the Elixir"** What is the final showdown? Does everyone live happily ever after or not?
Plot	Vader's troops chase the gang after the escape (94:28) The Death Star tracks the gang to the Rebel base (99:22) Plans to the Death Star reveal a weakness (99:55)	Luke chastises Han for leaving before the attack, gets ready to attack (102:00) Luke is assured by Obi-Wan's voice (104:50) The attack begins (106:35)	Vader joins the attack (108:30) Luke flies into the trenches (113:45) Han comes back, helps Luke (116:49) Luke destroys the Death Star, Vader escapes (117:14) Leia rewards Luke and Han (119:00)
On-screen Relationships (Outer Conflict)	Luke, Leia & Han Luke & Rebels	Luke & Han Luke & Leia Luke & Rebels Luke & Obi-Wan	Luke & Vader Luke & Han Luke, Leia & Han
Hero or Heroine's Needs (Inner Conflict)	Luke: Get Death Star plans to the Rebel base	Luke: Destroy Death Star	Luke: Destroy Death Star
Villain's Needs (Societal Conflict)	Destroy the Rebel base	Destroy the Rebel base	Kill Luke, Destroy the Rebel base

Film Deconstruction Chart – *The Wizard of Oz*

	ACT I		
Page / Sequence	**10 min / "Ordinary World"** What is the world of the story?	**20 min / "Call to Adventure"** What happens to get the story started?	**30 min / "Refusal of the Call"** How does the main character deny the need for change?
Plot	Kansas: Dorothy tries to explain to her family how she and Toto are tormented by Miss Gulch (3:45) Dorothy dreams of a place where there is no trouble (6:00)	Miss Gulch takes Toto away from Dorothy (8:00) After Toto escapes back, Dorothy decides they must run away (11:00)	Prof. Marvel tells Dorothy her family misses her (13:00) Dorothy runs back home during a twister (15:00)
On-screen Relationships (Outer Conflict)	Dorothy & Uncle, Aunt Dorothy & Zeke, Hunk, Hickory	Aunt Em, Uncle Henry & Miss Gulch	Dorothy & Prof. Marvel
Hero or Heroine's Needs (Inner Conflict)	Protect Toto, find a place where Dorothy can be appreciated	Protect Toto, find a place where Dorothy can be appreciated	Get home during the twister, protect Toto, find a place where Dorothy can be appreciated
Villain's Needs (Societal Conflict)	Miss Gulch: Destroy Toto	Destroy Toto	Destroy Toto

Film Deconstruction Chart – *The Wizard of Oz*

	ACT II – Part 1		
Page / Sequence	**40 min / "Meeting w/ Helper/Mentor"** Does the main character meet a mentor?	**50 min / "Crossing the First Threshold"** Does the main character enter a new world?	**60 min / "Tests, Helpers, Enemies"** Who/what are the new friends and obstacles our main character meets?
Plot	Dorothy's home lands in Oz (19:30) Dorothy meets Glinda, is shown that she has killed the Wicked Witch's sister (22:15) The Munchkins rejoice (25:00) The Ruby Slippers are put on Dorothy to protect her (30:00)	Dorothy goes off in search of the Wizard of Oz (33:00) – Her first steps on the Yellow Brick Road is the point where she crosses the first threshold Dorothy meets the Scarecrow, who has no brain and he joins her (39:00) Dorothy then meets the Tin Man, who has no heart and he joins her as well (47:30) Dorothy finally meets the Cowardly Lion, who has no courage and she convinces him to join along, too (52:00)	Dorothy and the Lion are poisoned by the Witch, but then saved by Glinda (56:45) Dorothy and her friends arrive at Oz, where the residents of the city pamper them for their meeting with the Wizard (59:00) The Witch frightens the city by threatening Dorothy over the sky (63:00)
On-screen Relationships (Outer Conflict)	Dorothy & Glinda Dorothy & Munchkins Dorothy & the Wicked Witch	Dorothy & Munchkins Dorothy & Scarecrow Dorothy & Tin Man Dorothy & Lion	Dorothy & Scarecrow, Tin Man & Lion Dorothy & the Wicked Witch Dorothy & Glinda Dorothy & the residents of Oz
Hero or Heroine's Needs (Inner Conflict)	Get home, protect Toto	Find Wizard to help Scarecrow to get a brain, Tin Man get a heart, and Lion get courage, get home, protect Toto	Find Wizard to help Scarecrow to get a brain, Tin Man get a heart, and Lion get courage, get home, protect Toto
Villain's Needs (Societal Conflict)	Wicked Witch: Destroy Dorothy & Toto, get Ruby Slippers	Destroy Dorothy & Toto, get Ruby Slippers	Destroy Dorothy & Toto, get Ruby Slippers

Film Deconstruction Chart – *The Wizard of Oz*

Page / Sequence	ACT II – Part 2		
	70 min / "Approach to Innermost Cave" How do the stakes go up? How does this send the main character in a new direction?	**80 min / "Ordeal & Flight"** How do things get bad enough to create a crisis?	**90 min / "Reward"** How does the crisis cause the main character to change?
Plot	Dorothy and her friends finally meet the Wizard (70:00) The requests of Dorothy and her friends are rejected by the Wizard until they prove themselves by retrieving the Witch's broomstick (72:40)	The Witch orders the Flying Monkeys to capture Dorothy and Toto (75:30) Witch finds slippers can only be removed if Dorothy is dead (77:10) Disguised as the Witch's guards Dorothy's friends rescue her (84:00) Dorothy saves Scarecrow and kills the Witch (86:27)	As the Wizard is rejecting the group again of their rewards he is discovered to be a fraud (89:11) The rewards are finally given to Dorothy's friends (92:00)
On-screen Relationships (Outer Conflict)	Dorothy & Scarecrow, Tin Man, Lion Dorothy & Wizard	Dorothy & Wicked Witch Dorothy & Scarecrow, Tin Man, Lion	Dorothy & Wizard Dorothy & Scarecrow, Tin Man, Lion
Hero or Heroine's Needs (Inner Conflict)	Retrieve the Wicked Witch's broomstick, help Scarecrow get a brain, Tin Man get a heart, and Lion get courage, get home, protect Toto	Retrieve the Wicked Witch's broomstick, help Scarecrow get a brain, Tin Man get a heart, and Lion get courage, get home, protect Toto	Return with the Wicked Witch's broomstick, help Scarecrow get a brain, Tin Man get a heart, and Lion get courage, get home, protect Toto
Villain's Needs (Societal Conflict)	Destroy Dorothy & Toto, get Ruby Slippers	Destroy Dorothy & Toto, get Ruby Slippers	

Copyright © 2011 by Marilyn Horowitz

139

Film Deconstruction Chart – *The Wizard of Oz*

	ACT III		
Page / Sequence	**100 min / "The Road Back"** What is the preparation for the final climax?	**110 min / "Resurrection"** How does the main character change?	**120 min / "Return w/ the Elixir"** What is the final showdown? Does everyone live happily ever after or not?
Plot	The Wizard loads Dorothy up in his balloon as they get ready to set off for Kansas (94:00) Dorothy jumps out of the balloon at the last moment to fetch Toto, but the Wizard is unable to stop the balloon's ascent and Dorothy is left behind in Oz (95:15)	As all seems lost, Glinda arrives in Oz (96:00) Glinda tells Dorothy that she could have gone home at any time—the Ruby Slippers are activated by clicking her heels together three times (97:30) Dorothy has a tough farewell with her friends (98:26)	Dorothy learns there's no place like home as she reunites with her family (99:00)
On-screen Relationships (Outer Conflict)	Dorothy & the Wizard Dorothy & Scarecrow, Tin Man, Lion	Dorothy & Scarecrow, Tin Man, Lion Dorothy & Glinda	Dorothy & her family
Hero or Heroine's Needs (Inner Conflict)	Get home, protect Toto	Find her heart's desire rests right at home	Return home
Villain's Needs (Societal Conflict)			

Step 4

Plot Your Screenplay

B. Deconstruction of

In the Line of Fire

Villain or Obstacle Deconstruction of *In the Line of Fire*

Watch *In the Line of Fire*, performing the same actions. This is a well-structured thriller that has a well-developed villain. Consider what your screenplay would be like if it were written with the same proportion of screen time allotted to your villain or obstacle. For example, *Wicked* is a book written from the Wicked Witch of the West's point of view.

Film Deconstruction Chart – *In the Line of Fire*

	ACT I		
Page / Sequence	**10 min / "Ordinary World"** What is the world of the story?	**20 min / "Call to Adventure"** What happens to get the story started?	**30 min / "Refusal of the Call"** How does the main character deny the need for change?
Plot	Frank & Al meet counterfeiters (2:36) Frank saves Al (5:10) Bar: Frank convinces Al not to quit (6:50) Frank discovers Shrine. Leary is watching (8:15–9:40)	Next day: Shrine is gone, except pic of Kennedy and Frank (10:57) Leary calls—game is afoot (12:33) Frank chases Leary (14:50) Briefing meeting, meets Lily and brushes against Bill (16:40) Frank asks Sam to get back to active service (18:48) Frank faces his age (19:40)	Leary is watching (20:48) Heart attack prank (21:20) Frank buys car magazine (23:00) Leary calls (24:00) Takes them to wrong house via wiretap (27:16) Chief of staff refuses to stop dinner (29:09) Leary keeps on creating weapon (29:40)
On-screen Relationships (Outer Conflict)	Frank & Al Frank & Leary	Frank & Leary Frank & Lily Frank & Sam Frank & Al	Frank w/ Secret Service agents Frank & Leary (on phone) **First Act turning point: wrong house, realizes Leary must be a pro**
Hero or Heroine's Needs (Inner Conflict)	Catch counterfeiters Save Al Be on time Save President, catch Leary	Save President, catch Leary, find love	Save President, catch Leary
Villain's Needs (Societal Conflict)	Kill President, involve Frank (he saw Frank through the window)	Kill President, involve Frank	Kill President, involve Frank

Film Deconstruction Chart – *In the Line of Fire*

	ACT II – Part 1		
Page / Sequence	**40 min / "Meeting w/ Helper/Mentor"** Does the main character meet a mentor?	**50 min / "Crossing the First Threshold"** Does the main character enter a new world?	**60 min / "Tests, Helpers, Enemies"** Who/what are the new friends and obstacles our main character meets?
Plot	French Embassy dinner Frank flirts with Lily (31:16) Leary deposits at Southwest Savings Bank. Bank representative asks too many questions (32:20) Frank asks Lily for a ride (34:00) Ice cream with Lily at Lincoln Memorial. Lily is interested (36:09) Leary shows up at Bank representative's house (36:40) Kills her and roommate (38:08) Leary calls at office, pushes more buttons on Frank (38:50)	Frank chases Leary, gets fingerprint (42:30) Leary finishes building gun (43:06) Leary is FBI, info can't be disclosed to Frank (43:34) Leary books flight to Los Angeles(45:50) Leary mails check for $40,000 (47:56)	Frank kisses Lily(51:21) Dallas—Leary watching (54:11) Leary sick (54:56) Frank and Lily get closer (56:17) Chicago—Frank thinks he hears gunshots (58:58) Leary popped a balloon(59:17)
On-screen Relationships (Outer Conflict)	Frank & Chief of Staff Frank & Leary Frank & Lily	Frank & Lily Frank gets sick at rally	Frank & Lily Frank & Chief of Staff Frank at rally
Hero or Heroine's Needs (Inner Conflict)	Save President, catch Leary, find love	Save President, catch Leary, find love	Save President, catch Leary, find love
Villain's Needs (Societal Conflict)	Kill President, reach out to Frank	Kill President, reach out to Frank	Kill President, reach out to Frank

Film Deconstruction Chart – *In the Line of Fire*

	ACT II – Part 2		
Page / Sequence	**70 min / "Approach to Innermost Cave"** How do the stakes go up? How does this send the main character in a new direction?	**80 min / "Ordeal & Flight"** How do things get bad enough to create a crisis?	**90 min / "Reward"** How does the crisis cause the main character to change?
Plot	Chief of Staff suspends Frank (1:00:41) Frank asks Sam to stay on Leary's case (1:02:54) Leary peeks at Frank inside bar (1:03:53) Leary calls Frank (1:04:19). Leary admits he popped balloon. Clue: Leary says, "Some die just because they come from Minneapolis." (1:05:29) Al has new lead to model builders (1:07:43) Professor of Design in Pasadena recollects he met Leary (1:07:53). He sends Frank and Al to Phoenix. With sketch they meet Walter Wycklan, who identifies Leary (1:08:57)	At Leary's home they find CIA (1:10:43). They discover Leary is assassin (1:11:43) Leary kills two innocents at lake (1:13:59) Briefing with CIA (1:14:55). Photo trials of Leary new look (1:15:27) Frank convinces Al not to resign (1:16:06) Leary calls (1:17:22). Leary reaches out to Frank (1:18:00) and gets mad	Frank and Al track Leary (1:20:42) Chase scene on roof (1:21:10) Leary saves Frank (1:25:00), kills Al (1:25:12) In hotel, FBI finds "Skellum" note (1:25:58) Frank at Bar. Leary calls (1:26:50) "Do you really have the guts to take a bullet, Frank?" (1:28:30) Frank checks Skellum as a person (1:28:50) Chief of Staff refuses to put off California speech (1:29:15)
On-screen Relationships (Outer Conflict)	Frank & Al investigating CIA	Frank & Leary Frank & Al	Frank & Lily (Frank has to beg Lily) Frank & Leary
Hero or Heroine's Needs (Inner Conflict)	Save President, catch Leary, find love	Save President, catch Leary, find love	Save President, **KILL Leary,** find love
Villain's Needs (Societal Conflict)	Kill President, reach out to Frank	Kill President, reach out to Frank	Kill President, reach out to Frank

Film Deconstruction Chart – *In the Line of Fire*

	ACT III		
Page / Sequence	**100 min / "The Road Back"** What is the preparation for the final climax?	**110 min / "Resurrection"** How does the main character change?	**120 min / "Return w/ the Elixir"** What is the final showdown? Does everyone live happily ever after or not?
Plot	Frank asks Lily to be put on advance team (1:30:23) Intercut: Frank & Leary preparing Leary arrives at Hotel (1:35:45) Frank beats up bellboy, thrown off detail (1:36:13) Leary checks in as James Carney (1:36:54) Frank gets dinner guest list (and checks) (1:37:58) Lily receives call that Frank is dismissed (1:39:29)	Frank mourns Kennedy w/ Lily (1:41:25) At airport, Frank realizes that "SKELLUM" is the phone number for Southwest Savings (1:44:33) Frank discovers previous account representative is dead (1:46:20) Frank starts tracking down Leary's account (2nd Turning Point) Leary passes security check (1:48:48) Leary assembles gun (1:49:28)	Frank finds out Leary's alias name (1:51:55) Leary loads gun (1:52:21) Leary spots Frank (1:52:58) Frank spots Leary, takes bullet, saves President (1:53:31) Leary takes Frank hostage (1:54:08) Leary stops elevator, puts out lights (1:55:29) Frank "aim high" (1:57:49) Frank takes out Leary (1:58:34) Leary refuses Frank's help and dies (1:59:13) Frank is a hero (2:00:35) Frank retires (2:00:49) Frank at home listens to Leary's last message (2:01:42). Frank moves on. At Lincoln Memorial together with Lily (2:03:47)
On-screen Relationships (Outer Conflict)	Frank & Lily Leary on his own	Frank on his own Leary on his own	Frank & Leary Frank & Lily Frank & Sam
Hero or Heroine's Needs (Inner Conflict)	Save President, **KILL Leary,** find love	Save President, **KILL Leary,** find love	Save President, **KILL Leary,** find love Move on
Villain's Needs (Societal Conflict)	Kill President, kill Frank	Kill President, kill Frank	Kill President, kill Frank

Step 4

Plot Your Screenplay

Part III.

Outline Your Screenplay Using the

Deconstruction Chart

Outline Your Screenplay

Now you will create an outline of your screenplay using the Deconstruction Chart.

You've done the work of preparing your characters, picked a Premise-Question, learned how to use the Mythic Journey Map and the Three Levels of Conflict.

This new chart combines the Mythic Journey Map and the Three Levels of Conflict so you can easily visualize how they work in tandem.

The goal is to continuously identify what is preventing your main character from realizing his or her dream at every moment of the entire screenplay.

Creating Your Screenplay Using the Mythic Journey Map and the Three Levels of Conflict

Write Your Premise-Question Here:

_____

Page / Sequence	ACT I		
	10 min / "Ordinary World" What is the world of the story?	20 min / "Call to Adventure" What happens to get the story started?	30 min / "Refusal of the Call" How does the main character deny the need for change?
Plot			
On-screen Relationships (Outer Conflict)			
Hero or Heroine's Needs (Inner Conflict)			
Villain's Needs (Societal Conflict)			

Creating Your Screenplay Using the Mythic Journey Map and the Three Levels of Conflict

Page / Sequence	ACT II — Part 1		
	40 min / "Meeting w/ Helper/Mentor" Does the main character meet a mentor?	50 min / "Crossing the First Threshold" Does the main character enter a new world?	60 min / "Tests, Helpers, Enemies" Who/what are the new friends and obstacles our main character meets?
Plot			
On-screen Relationships (Outer Conflict)			
Hero or Heroine's Needs (Inner Conflict)			
Villain's Needs (Societal Conflict)			

Creating Your Screenplay Using the Mythic Journey Map and the Three Levels of Conflict

	ACT II — Part 2		
Page / Sequence	70 min / "Approach to Innermost Cave" How do the stakes go up? How does this send the main character in a new direction?	80 min / "Ordeal & Flight" How do things get bad enough to create a crisis?	90 min / "Reward" How does the crisis cause the main character to change?
Plot			
On-screen Relationships (Outer Conflict)			
Hero or Heroine's Needs (Inner Conflict)			
Villain's Needs (Societal Conflict)			

Creating Your Screenplay Using the Mythic Journey Map and the Three Levels of Conflict

	ACT III		
Page / Sequence	**100 min / "The Road Back"** What is the preparation for the final climax?	**110 min / "Resurrection"** How does the main character change?	**120 min / "Return w/ the Elixir"** What is the final showdown? Does everyone live happily ever after or not?
Plot			
On-screen Relationships (Outer Conflict)			
Hero or Heroine's Needs (Inner Conflict)			
Villain's Needs (Societal Conflict)			

Step 4

Plot Your Screenplay

Part IV.

Begin to Write Your Screenplay Using

the Mythic Journey Map Worksheet

The Mythic Journey Map Worksheet

The Mythic Journey Map Worksheet forms a bridge between structuring your story and writing the screenplay.

Now that you have an outline, the real fun begins. The Mythic Journey Map Worksheet will help you get a fresh angle on the outline you've already done. Your next step is to transfer your outline from the Deconstruction Chart to the Mythic Journey Map Worksheet.

As you write, describe the action like this:

"Frank and Al nail the counterfeiters who try to kill Al. Frank waits for the right moment, then shoots the bad guys and saves his partner."

Then ask yourself what the point of the scene is—for example, "I want us to know Frank can be ruthless, a match for Leary." By knowing the dramatic point of each scene, you will become more focused and make better choices.

This process of transferring also allows you to "see" how your screenplay will actually look when it's finished. The shift from a horizontal list to a vertical one will help you get a new angle on your story, both literally and figuratively. On the next page is an example from one of my students of how to use this worksheet:

	ACT I		
Page / Sequence	10 min / "Ordinary World" What is the world of the story?	20 min / "Call to Adventure" What happens to get the story started?	30 min / "Refusal of the Call" How does the main character deny the need for change?
Plot	Frank & Al meet counterfeiters (2:36) Frank saves Al (5:10) Bar: Frank convinces Al not to quit (6:50) Frank discovers Shrine. Leary is watching (8:15-9:40)	Next day: Shrine is gone, except pic of Ken-nedy and Frank.(10:57) Leary Calls-game is afoot(12:33) Frank chases Leary(14:50) Briefing meeting, meets Lily and brushes against Bill(16:40) Frank asks Sam to get back to active ser-vice(18:48) Frank faces his age (19:40)	Leary is watching(20:48) Heart attack prank(21:20) Frank buys car magazine(23:00) Leary calls (24:00) takes them to wrong house via wire tap (27:16) Chief of staff refuses to stop dinner(29:09) Leary keeps on creating weapon(29:40)
Onscreen (Relationships)	Frank & Al Frank and Leary	Frank & Leary Frank & Lily Frank & Sam Frank & Al	Frank w/ Secret Service agents Frank & Leary (on phone) **1st Act turning point: wrong house, realizes Leary must be a pro**
Hero/Heroine's Need	Catch counterfeiters Save Al Be on time Save President, catch Leary	Save President, catch Leary, find love	Save President, catch Leary
Villain's Need	Kill President, involve Frank (he saw Frank through the window)	Kill President, involve Frank	Kill President, involve Frank

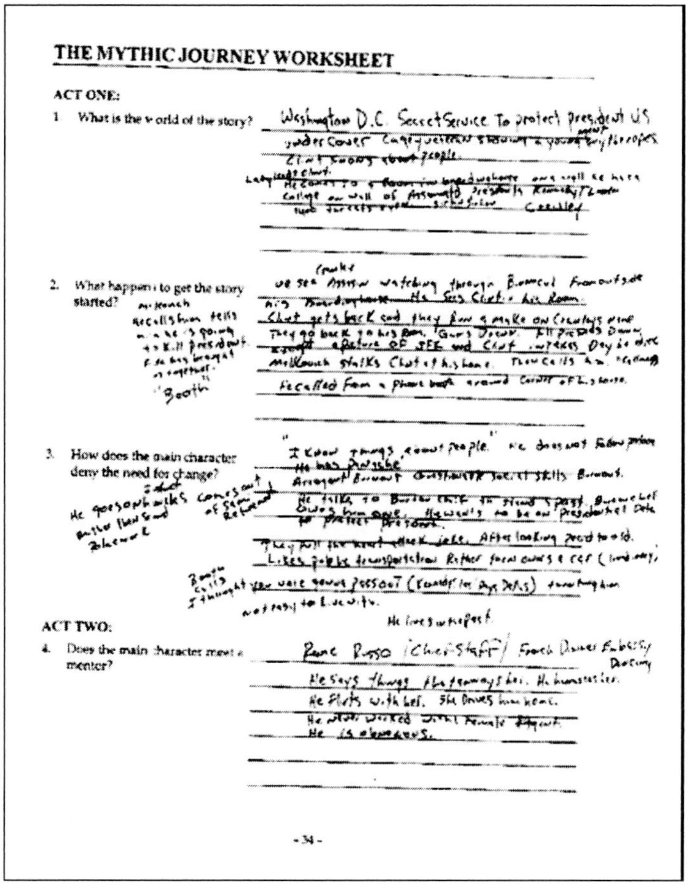
THE MYTHIC JOURNEY WORKSHEET
ACT ONE:
1 What is the world of the story?
Washington D.C. Secret Service To protect president US
2. What happens to get the story started?
"Booth"
3. How does the main character deny the need for change?
"I know things about people."
After looking good to old.
ACT TWO:
4. Does the main character meet a mentor?
Rene Russo (Chief-Staff)
He flirts with her. She drives him home.
- 34 -

If we can pretend that the film my student was writing was *In the Line of Fire*, the filled out Worksheet is a good example of what happens during the transfer process.

As the student transferred the info from the Mythic Journey Map to the Worksheet, he began to get little ideas and images, fragments of dialogue and ideas, which he wrote in the margins next to the form.

This is the magic part of this System. As you write your outline, you will get glimpses of how your script would look if it were already a film. You may get ideas for new scenes and mentally "hear" snatches of dialogue. When you can imagine something that clearly, it will feel like it already exists. And as I said earlier, "remembering" is easier than making things up.

The process that happens here is really a trick wherein you get your mind to act "as if" all the events in your film have already happened and you are simply recording them as you would a diary entry!

You can see how it will be easy to fill in what you feel is still missing from your outline, and to begin writing scenes. You should be raring to get started when you're done with this exercise. Good Luck and Happy Writing!

Study the completed Mythic Journey Map Worksheet on the next page, pretending that you're looking at an outline for a screenplay.

THE MYTHIC JOURNEY WORKSHEET

ACT ONE:

1. What is the world of the story? _Washington D.C. Secret Service. To protect president U.S._
under cover. Congregation staring a young boy for cops.
Clint knows about people.

2. What happens to get the story started?

3. How does the main character deny the need for change?

ACT TWO:

4. Does the main character meet a mentor?
Rene Russo (Chief-Staff) French Dinner Embassy
He says things that annoy she. He humorsice.
He flirts with her. She drives him home.
He never worked with female agent.
He is obnoxious.

THE MYTHIC JOURNEY WORKSHEET

ACT TWO:

5. Does the main character enter a new world?

John Malkovich teases him is across in park
Clut sees him across the street. chases him down street
Clut is outof shape. Gets fingerprints C-12
Canthese Classified.

Clut is furious when things Don't go his way

6. Who/what are the new friends and obstacles our main character meets?

Rene Russo / Malkovich

Afterwards They Kiss in theater

then go to Room inner set (Prop & liquor stuff
then get the
Call to Another Kill.

7. How do the stakes go up? How does this send the main character in a new direction?

Now They are involved (Clut/Rene
He is emotionally involved wishes her to be careful
Clut is set at presidential Rally Guard S
he mistakes for a gun fake alarm Russ Rally.
He may be to old to stand a post.

He is told by Secret Service & chef of staff he is
thrown off Detail. For being humilated And
Clut is a Dick. Should Retire. His pinew chief
wants him to Retire. He is to old for physi.

8. How do things get bad enough to create a crisis?

He is allowed to stay on Booth Detail but not
on Presidential Detail

Allistaff
 is to pay   _Malkovich wants to Kill president_   To purchase sad Program

"Playing the game"   its a game   Malkovich is an office
                                              Clut is on Defense

Cluts partner stands up and they
get a Composite Sketch. They start Doing
police work. Tracking him Down they
Track him to an address of a home

-35- looks abandonment. CIA C-12 people
Leary   _show up we find out_
                               he is an government
                               Assasin/protestor.

THE MYTHIC JOURNEY WORKSHEET

ACT TWO:

9. How does the crisis cause the main character to change?

[handwritten] malchleary is CIA assassin. He need to get there he has killed all his friends. They go to all his possible Disguises & whereabals. Tell him by his eyes. However he talks to partner about blowup he wants to quit Clint talks him into staying & he gets killed. He tells malkovich he knows it is Leery. You slit your friends throat.

They chase malkovich through an Ally, up a Roof Hurtling over a roof rope. malkovic has him hanging by a thread throws him onto Balcony. Then kills Partner Al.

ACT THREE:

10. What is the preparation for the final climax?

[handwritten] Revenge for Al. Good Police work Finds books. He killed records of 50 Thousand transaction. Jim Carrey for Dinner

11. How does the main character change?

[handwritten] He has gone from wanting to protect to being an ATESSin. He talks to Rene Russo to get on her Advanced Detail. He says "Please for first time" in Rene Russo. Coming to Bonaventure Hotel to Rene Russo He admits he didn't react when JFK was shot. He holds her hand and admits now that it would be alright with me If I'd take Bullet.

12. What is the final showdown? Do they live happily ever after or not?

[handwritten] weeks int Bonaventure Hotel presidential Room. Clint is shaked out. Malkovic is Ready to murder president. wears a Disguise. Malkovic Comes Running, Malkovic Removed Sharpshooters on Roof. Details of officers & Secret Service. Malkovic Smuggles his bullets of Plastic Gun in another Alias. Thousand Guests at California victory Fund. Clint takes Bullet saving president. malkovich takes him as prisoner. up elevator. He Retires lives happily ever after. He Loves things.

(Mythic Journey Map Worksheet prepared by Mark Stogo)

The Mythic Journey Map Worksheet

Transfer your own work for the Deconstruction Chart to the Mythic Journey Map Worksheet below.

ACT ONE:

1. What is the world of the story?

_____
_____
_____
_____
_____
_____

2. What happens to get the story started?

_____
_____
_____
_____
_____
_____

3. How does the main character deny the need for change?

_____
_____
_____
_____
_____

ACT TWO:

4. Does the main character meet a mentor?

_____
_____
_____
_____
_____

The Mythic Journey Map Worksheet

ACT TWO (Cont'd):

5. Does the main character enter a new world?

6. Who/what are the new friends and obstacles our main character meets?

7. How do the stakes go up? How does this send the main character in a new direction?

8. How do things get bad enough to create a crisis?

The Mythic Journey Map Worksheet

ACT TWO (Cont'd):

9. How does the crisis cause the
    main character to change?

    _____
    _____
    _____
    _____
    _____
    _____

ACT THREE:

10. What is the preparation for the
    final climax?

    _____
    _____
    _____
    _____
    _____
    _____

11. How does the main character
    change?

    _____
    _____
    _____
    _____
    _____

12. What is the final showdown?
    Does everyone live happily ever
    after or not?

    _____
    _____
    _____
    _____
    _____

STEP 5

How to Write Your Screenplay in 10 Weeks

Congratulations! If you are reading this, you are about to write your screenplay in 10 weeks

Before You Begin

I recommend that you open your calendar and schedule as many one-hour writing sessions as you can each week. I find that if you make appointments, you are much more likely to keep them. If the time arrives and you aren't in the mood, don't skip it. Watch a part of a movie, read a screenplay you admire, do research if your story requires it. In other words, get yourself inspired.

Don't believe that old chestnut about waiting for inspiration to strike. Inspiration is not something that comes to you, it's something you have to woo, and sometimes chase. A favorite technique of mine is to begin copying someone else's script. After less than a page, I start rewriting their material, and then know what I want to do with my own.

Write, *"Don't Get It Right, Get It Written,"* down and tape it to your computer, or make the phrase your screensaver. This is the key to getting the draft done. Don't look back once you have started. Force yourself to go forward until you type, "Fade Out."

How To Get Started

The first scene you write should be the scene you feel most attracted to. This is not a whimsical suggestion. After working with many writers, I understand that the process of creation is not linear. A paradox here: even though we have organized your screenplay from beginning to end, this doesn't mean you have to write it this way. One of the most liberating things about The System is that it sets you free to write in any order that appeals to you. And you can't get lost because you have a map!

Here are some examples of how to write:

Write in order: Start with Scene 1. Check off each scene as you complete it. Make notes in your log about where, when and how you wrote. Give yourself a pat on the back, and then go earn another one.

If that doesn't feel right, here are some examples of how other people do it. Find one you like or try your own. The only measure of success is whether or not you are producing pages.

Write out of order: One of my students challenged this and decided he would write by sequence, but out of order. It was a thriller about a soccer mom who used to be in the CIA and is called back for one last job. So he wrote sequence 3, the "Refusal of the Call" from the Mythic Journey Map Worksheet, then sequence 6, "Test, Helpers, Enemies" and so on. When he reassembled the sequences, they fit together as if he had written them in order!

Draw your scene: Another student made drawings of the scenes he could "see" in his mind's eye and then wrote the dialogue. His story is a drama about a family coping with divorce. When he got a pile he looked at his outline and placed them on a Deconstruction Chart and then filled in what was missing. I think of this approach as using the "holes" to find the "wholes." Seeing any part of a script is better than seeing none.

Expand the Mythic Journey Map Worksheet: A student used the Mythic Journey Map Worksheet form to write a "treatment," a longer more detailed synopsis with bits of dialogue.

Write as if you were writing fiction: This means you can write long descriptions and tell what your characters think and feel. Then convert this into screenplay form. You won't be able to use most of what you write, but writers have to write. Sometimes the screenplay form is too rigid for the first round of creating.

I will also often write the climactic sequence in Act 3 first. It's like having dessert first. If you have your cake first, then you don't rush through your food to get to the good part.

It's up to you. For once, do it the way it feels best. Don't let anyone tell you how you like to do it. Let this first draft be an exploration of both your script and your creative process.

But in order to be free, you MUST keep a written record. In the log provided on the following pages, write something that you did that relates to your screenplay every day, seven days a week. Writers feel that they are not working unless they are actually writing, but the truth is that we are working all the time. Every film you watch, every note you take, every thought you have about your script counts. Once you see how much time you actually spend working on your script, you will be encouraged to spend even more time!

A Few Writing Tips

Plan out your writing schedule with a friend, teacher or partner and have them check up on you.

Make appointments with yourself and **keep them.**

Use a timer.

Try to write one scene per sitting.

Tape your Premise-Question to your computer.

And remember: **Don't get it right—get it written!**

Writing Timeline

This timeline will help you stay on track. Transfer the deadlines to your PDA, Blackberry, or wherever you schedule.

Week	Task	Steps/Pages	Activity	Due Date	Completed
Week 1	Prep	Steps 1-2	Complete exercises for Steps 1-2		☐
Week 2	Prep	Steps 3-4	Complete exercises for Steps 3-4		☐
Week 3	Writing	pp 1 - 15	Write		☐
Week 4	Writing	pp 16 - 30	Write		☐
Week 5	Writing	pp 31 - 45	Write		☐
Week 6	Writing	pp 46 - 60	Write		☐
Week 7	Writing	pp 61 – 75	Write		☐
Week 8	Writing	pp 76 – 90	Write		☐
Week 9	Writing	pp 90 – 105	Write		☐
Week 10	Writing	pp 106 - 120	Write		☐

The Importance of Keeping a Log

Keeping a log helps you to keep track of your time and to plan. Sit down and figure out when you have time to write as your life is now. Don't be dismayed when you realize your life is much fuller than you thought. This is a good thing—it will provide material for your next screenplay!

Now that you realize that you will have to squeeze writing into your life, the log provided will help you find the time to write your screenplay.

Here are some suggestions that will help you with your planning:

One of my students gets up an hour early and puts an hour in at a coffee shop close to work. Starbucks is a real boon to writers.

Another puts on her makeup before she goes to the gym, which frees up 20 minutes before work.

A stay-at-home dad in suburbia bought a pre-fab shed and put it at the far end of his property to get away from the family. He hired a babysitter, and works for 45 minutes while his infant naps in the afternoon.

Another has a night job, and she comes home at 2:00am. She takes a shower, pretends she's just gotten up and gets her stuff done between 2:00am and 5:00am.

Your creativity isn't limited to your writing. Finding time to write often takes as much ingenuity as plotting.

Writing Log

WRITING LOG

Week	Task	Steps/Pages	Activity	Completed
Week 1				
Mon	Write scene 1	Pages completed	Writing, watched movie, reading screenplays, talking to partner, other related activities. was it fun?	☐
Tue				☐
Wed				☐
Thur				☐
Fri				☐
Sat				☐
Sun				☐

WRITING LOG

Week	Task	Steps/Pages	Activity	Completed
Week 2				
Mon				☐
Tue				☐
Wed				☐
Thur				☐
Fri				☐
Sat				☐
Sun				☐

WRITING LOG

Week	Task	Steps/Pages	Activity	Completed
Week 3				
Mon				☐
Tue				☐
Wed				☐
Thur				☐
Fri				☐
Sat				☐
Sun				☐

WRITING LOG

Week	Task	Steps/Pages	Activity	Completed
Week 4				
Mon				☐
Tue				☐
Wed				☐
Thur				☐
Fri				☐
Sat				☐
Sun				☐

WRITING LOG

Week	Task	Steps/Pages	Activity	Completed
Week 5				
Mon				☐
Tue				☐
Wed				☐
Thur				☐
Fri				☐
Sat				☐
Sun				☐

WRITING LOG

Week	Task	Steps/Pages	Activity	Completed
Week 6				
Mon				☐
Tue				☐
Wed				☐
Thur				☐
Fri				☐
Sat				☐
Sun				☐

WRITING LOG

Week	Task	Steps/Pages	Activity	Completed
Week 7				
Mon				☐
Tue				☐
Wed				☐
Thur				☐
Fri				☐
Sat				☐
Sun				☐

WRITING LOG

Week	Task	Steps/Pages	Activity	Completed
Week 8				
Mon				☐
Tue				☐
Wed				☐
Thur				☐
Fri				☐
Sat				☐
Sun				☐

WRITING LOG

Week	Task	Steps/Pages	Activity	Completed
Week 9				
Mon				☐
Tue				☐
Wed				☐
Thur				☐
Fri				☐
Sat				☐
Sun				☐

WRITING LOG

Week	Task	Steps/Pages	Activity	Completed
Week 10				
Mon				☐
Tue				☐
Wed				☐
Thur				☐
Fri				☐
Sat				☐
Sun				☐

STEP 6
Spec-Script Format Guide

SCREENPLAY FORMAT: A BRIEF MANUAL OF STYLE

NOTE: The mission of this manual is to provide a
          coherent breakdown of the rules that define the
          "industry standard." The rules were developed
          so that directors, writers, producers and actors
          could "talk" to each other.

          Remember that the purpose of these rules is to
          provide writers with the best tools to
          communicate their visions. Don't rebel -- sell!

          Good luck.

<u>**YOUR SCRIPT TITLE HERE**</u>

by

The Author

Your Address
Your phone number

This guide will allow you to set up your script in
MS Word without having to use special software. On the
next page you will find a list of the specific styles
used in formatting a screenplay.

BASIC FORMATTING:

Typeface: Your entire screenplay should be printed in 12-
point Courier or (for Windows users) Courier New, the
same font as on this page. This is equivalent to:

        10-cpi Courier (found on electric typewriters)
        12-point "Pica" found on old manual typewriters

Margins: Give each page as much "white space" as possible.
This makes it a more pleasing "read." Here are the
industry guidelines:

        A. Left Margin: 1.5 inches
        B. Right Margin: 1.25 inches
        C. Top & Bottom Margins: 1.0 inches

These are the margins used in this manual.

Tabs: Set these tabs from your ruler line. The
measurements here start at the left margin, not at the
edge of the paper. This is standard on most word
processors.

        A. Dialogue: 1 inch (both sides)
        B. Parentheticals: 1.75 inches
        C. Character Slugs: Indented 3.5 inches from
                                page edge
        D. Optical Directions: Flush right

See the example below:

                    TIFFANY
          What's your secret with men?

                     EMMA
          Scorn, disinterest, perfume.

                    TIFFANY
          Well, it sure seems to work.

                                        DISSOLVE TO:

<u>Styles</u>: Below are styles you can create in MS Word to
help you format your screenplay properly. Use them or
create new ones of your own. You may need help if you
not familiar with creating styles in MS Word.

All of these styles start with a base style of <u>Normal</u>,
use font type <u>Courier New</u>, and have a <u>font size</u> of <u>12 pts</u>.

Style Name	**MS Word Format for the Style**
Spec Bullet	Indent: Left: 0", Hanging: 0.25", Space Before: 12 pt, Bulleted + Level: 1 + Aligned at: 0.25" + Tab after: 0.5" + Indent at: 0.5"
Spec Cover Name/Address	Indent: Left: 3.65", Space Before: 250 pt
Spec Cover Title	Underline, Centered, Space Before: 190 pt
Spec Cover Title 2	Underline, Centered
Spec Cover Title Center	Centered, Space Before: 12 pt
Spec Text	Space Before: 12 pt
Spec Text Bold	Bold, Underline, Space Before: 12 pt
Spec Text Ind	Indent: Left: 0.5", Space Before: 12 pt
Spec Text Ind Hang	Indent: Left: 0.5", Hang: 0.35", Space Before: 12 pt
Spec Text Ind Small	Indent: Left: 0.12", Space Before: 12 pt
Dialog	Indent: Left: 1", Right: 1"
Dialog Head	Indent: Left: 2", Space Before: 12 pt, Keep with next
Dialog Ind	Indent: Left: 1.5", Right: 1"

<u>Line Spacing</u>: Single space at all times. Double-space
between copy blocks and scenes.

<u>Justification</u>: Only use left justification, except for
the optical directions noted above. Never use full
justification.

<u>Page Numbers</u>: Upper right hand corner, followed by a
period. The cover page and page one have no numbers.

<u>Bold, italics, fancy fonts</u>: Never. Underlines are to be
used as indicated in the following sections.

<u>Spelling and Grammar</u>: Proper spelling and grammar is essential. Dialogue can be written in slang.

<u>Sides</u>: The screenplay pages are always only single-sided.

<u>Paper</u>: Use standard weight (20 lb), three-hole punch paper.

<u>Covers</u>: Use plain cardstock with a three-hole punch. Do not put <u>anything</u> on the front or back cover. White or black covers only.

<u>Binding</u>: Always use #5 or #6 brads through the top and bottom holes of the three-hole punch. Never put a brad through the middle - everyone will know right away that you're an amateur.

<u>Length</u>: Try for between 90 and 120 pages. If possible, do not exceed 120 pages.

On the following pages are more detailed formatting instructions.

SCENE SLUGS:

Define the scene. All locations require a scene slug.
You cannot cut to a new location without using one. See
the example below:

INT. BILL'S BAR -- NIGHT

There are three parts to each slug: the location type
(INT. or EXT.), the description (BILL'S BAR), and the
time of day (DAY, NIGHT, EVE., MORNING).

— Note that scene slugs ARE ALWAYS IN ALL CAPS.

— All slugs need to be followed by at least one line of
  description. Example:

INT. BILL'S BAR -- NIGHT

A low-end dive filled with A SEAMY CROWD.

— Don't number your scenes.

— Don't leave a scene slug "floating" at the bottom of
  your page.

Location Type: Use INT. for "Interior" and EXT. for
"exterior." If moving to a different part of an
established interior location, you must reslug with INT.,
since this usually involves building another set.

Don't repeat "EXT." when moving to a different part of a
single exterior location. Just note the type of setting.

A car is an EXT. when it's on the road and an INT. when
it's in a garage.

What's a train, plane, or big ship? An INT. if your
scene is inside the vehicle, an EXT. if it's on the deck,
the roof, or otherwise outside the vehicle.

Location Description:

<u>Go from the general to the specific</u>. For example:

INT. MONA'S APARTMENT - BEDROOM -- NIGHT

<u>Not</u>:

INT. BEDROOM IN MONA'S APARTMENT -- NIGHT

<u>Avoid redundancies</u>. For example:

EXT. MONA'S APARTMENT BUILDING -- NIGHT

<u>Not</u>:

EXT. OUTSIDE MONA'S APARTMENT BUILDING -- NIGHT

Since you've already slugged the location as an EXT., you don't need to start your description with an "OUTSIDE."

<u>Cars don't exist in emptiness</u>. A car description should include where it is. For example:

EXT. CAR ON HIGHWAY

<u>Not</u>:

EXT. CAR

<u>No camera directions</u>. The director will ignore them anyway.

<u>Establishing shots</u> should be written in the scene text. For example:

EXT. NEW YORK CITY -- DAY

Establishing.

Time of Day:

Start with a space after the description, followed by a double dash, followed by the time of day in broad terms: DAY, NIGHT, EVE. Don't use specific times, e.g., 4:00 PM, unless it's germane to the story.

Interiors don't need the time of day unless there's a window or door to the exterior.

If you've established the time of day for a location, you
can use -- LATER if the same location is returned to in
the next scene. For example:

EXT. STREET CORNER -- DAY

Bill hangs out drinking beer. He passes out.

EXT. STREET CORNER -- LATER

Bill wakes up.

Keep in mind, however, that if the time of day changes
(if Bill wakes up at NIGHT), you have to indicate the new
time.

Don't time-slug a scene CONTINUOUS or SAME TIME if it
takes place right after the previous scene. Such
temporal continuity is assumed.

Flashback/Fantasy/Year: This is the fourth part of the
scene slug, and not always used. If you have a flashback
or a fantasy, or are indicating a specific year, you have
to put it in parentheses after the time of day. For
example:

EXT. NEW YORK CITY -- DAY (1900)

INT. BILL'S APARTMENT -- NIGHT (FLASHBACK)

INT. BILL'S APARTMENT -- MORNING (DREAM SEQUENCE)

Acceptable indicators include (FLASHBACK), (DREAM
SEQUENCE), (DREAM), (FANTASY).

Always add (REALITY) or (PRESENT DAY) to the slug that
brings us back to the here-and-now.

DESCRIPTION:

Less is more. Pare everything down. For example:

> INT. BAR -- NIGHT
>
> Dim, greasy. BILL, 20s, gaunt and ugly, sits at the bar.

Not:

> INT. BAR -- NIGHT
>
> A bar with dim lighting and a greasy atmosphere. BILL, in his 20s, a gaunt and ugly man, sits at the bar.

Keep all copy blocks four lines long or less. Thick blocks of description encourage readers to skip ahead.

Write in short, simple sentences. Avoid frequent use of the word "and." Don't leave out articles, e.g., "the," "a," "his," etc.

Don't use camera directions. Except for FADE IN, FADE OUT, avoid describing camera angles and scene transitions.

Don't bring "US" into your screenplay. Don't use phrases like "We see..." or "We realize..."

Always describe your setting before you describe characters or their actions.

Don't duplicate information from your scene slugs. For example:

INT. DINER -- DAY

Mary enters.

Not:

INT. DINER -- DAY

Mary enters the diner.

<u>Don't describe a location twice.</u>

<u>Don't describe the furniture</u> unless it's essential to a
character or to the story. Bad example:

>   INT. LIVING ROOM -- DAY
>
>   A gorgeous, spacious living room with coat rack,
>   television, sofa, and ornate loveseat. Marie sits
>   on the loveseat, watching television.

Good example:

INT. LIVING ROOM -- DAY

Gorgeous. Marie sits on the ornate loveseat, watching
television.

<u>Never begin your scene with a pronoun.</u> Always be
specific about who you're referring to.

<u>Music Cues</u>: Don't include music cues. You can note that
music is present in a scene, and even the <u>type</u> of music
being played.

VERB USAGE:

Keep your verbs in the active, present tense. Avoid "ing" words. Bad example:

Bill is eating his breakfast.

Good example:

Bill eats his breakfast.

The Verb "to be": Try to avoid it if possible. For example:

Laura sits at her desk.

Not:

Laura is sitting at her desk.

Starts/Begins to: Avoid this too. For example:

Larry eats his lobster.

Not:

Larry begins to eat his lobster.

ACTION:

<u>Don't get too elaborate</u>. But try to keep it short and to
the point. Action screenplays are an exception to this.

<u>Use "bullet" sentences</u>. You can even put them on
separate lines. For example:

>   Agent Trent sees the fugitive running.
>
>   Chases him.
>
>   Pulls his gun.
>
>   SHOOTS him dead.

<u>Important actions and sounds</u>: These should always be in
CAPS. For example: the phone RINGS, the dog BARKS.

Important actions would include: Mark SHOOTS Frank. Jack
CRASHES his car into a brick wall. John PLUNGES the knife
into Don's chest.

<u>Separate action from dialogue</u>: Don't put character
action within dialogue blocks. Write it as a separate
description.

Bad example:

> EMMA
> You know, Janey, you really anger me
> when you do that.
>   (She pulls out a gun)
> Maybe it's just cheaper to kill you.

Good example:

> EMMA
> You know, Janey, you really anger me
> when you do that.

She pulls out a gun.

> EMMA (CONT'D)
> Maybe it's just cheaper to kill you.

CHARACTERS:

Character Names: Vary the names of your character. For example, a script that includes a ROB and a ROBBIE or an ANDREAS and an ELIAS is hard to follow.

Character Descriptions: When you introduce a character, always put their name in CAPS. From then on, only use proper case (Jack, not jack or JACK).

— Briefly describe him/her by type and function.

— Don't be too specific about his/her age or physical characteristics, unless these elements are plot-critical. Use an age range if you need to.

Character Subtext: Don't use it. Only describe what we see and actions that characters perform.

You can describe an emotional state, however. For example: "Mona is sad." But not: "Mona is sad over having lost her life to that loser Bill."

Business: This is what a character does in a scene, such as lighting a cigarette or fidgeting with their wedding ring.

Again, less is more.

PHONES:

<u>When two people are speaking over the phone:</u> First, slug
both locations for the first line or so of dialogue.
Then add the INTERCUT line and treat it as the same
location. For example:

INT. BILL'S APARTMENT -- NIGHT

The phone RINGS. Bill wakes up groggily, picks up the
phone.

                        BILL
        What?

INT. MONA'S APARTMENT -- NIGHT

Mona sits by the phone, smoking.

                        MONA
        Bill, got a minute?

INTERCUT AS NEEDED

                        BILL
        What is your problem? I'm working on
        a hangover.

                        MONA
        Sorry, Bill. Can I borrow fifty
        bucks?

NOTE: I personally hate it when people talk on the phone
in a script. Try to get them face-to-face. If not, a
better choice is:

INT. MONA'S APARTMENT -- NIGHT

Mona picks up the phone, dials.

                        MONA
        Bill, got a minute?
           (Listens)
        You got a hangover? Bummer. Listen,
        can I borrow fifty bucks?

MISCELLANEOUS RULES FOR DESCRIPTION:

<u>Numbers</u>: In description, spell out numbers zero through nine, but use numerals for 10 and above.

In dialogue, write out <u>all</u> spoken numbers, except years. Years are always expressed in numerals.

<u>Don't leave abbreviated words</u> that end with periods ("Mr.," "Dr.," "Sgt.," etc.) dangling at the end of lines. Move the abbreviated word down to the next line, to link up with the word it modifies.

<u>Hyphenates</u>: Don't hyphenate words at the ends of lines.

<u>Page Endings</u>: Don't end a page in mid-sentence. Always end a page on a complete sentence.

<u>Titles</u>: Titles of movies, TV shows or publications like <u>Gone with the Wind</u> or <u>Time Magazine</u> should always be underlined, whether in dialogue or in the description.

<u>Montages</u>: A montage is the optical blending of various scenes, usually used as an ellipse between two important scenes. Use the following format:

MONTAGE:

George in bed, George sitting up, George running around.

<u>Text on a computer screen, text in a newspaper, etc.</u> Keep this to a minimum. Drop to a separate line, and use ON or IN, followed by a description of what the text is written on, followed by a colon.

Drop to the next line, and write out the text in quotes. For short text, use CAPS. For example:

ON SCREEN:

THIS IS THE END OF YOUR WORLD.

For brief letters or notes, you can get away with the "The note reads:" followed by the text. For example:

The note reads: Sorry, don't mean to be a pest.

<u>DIALOGUE</u>:

<u>Keep actions out of parentheticals</u> except when necessary.
It slows down the read. For example:

Jane sits down.

                    JANE
          Men: you can't live with them, you
          can't kill them.

NOT:

                    JANE
               (sits down)
          Men: you can't live with them, you
          can't kill them.

Keep dialogue sharp. Keep ellipses (...) and dashes to a
minimum. They are difficult for an actor to interpret:
how long is a dash?

<u>Use parentheticals</u> when a character changes who she or he
is talking to. For example:

                    JILL
          Give me a break!
               (to Mary)
          He's always like that after a few
          beers.

<u>If a character pauses</u> for a significant length of time,
reslug the dialogue. For example:

                    JANE
          I don't know.

Jane leans back.

                    JANE (CONT'D)
          Maybe I should just kill you ...

<u>Keep it short</u>. Long monologues are difficult to watch,
unless you're watching <u>Hamlet</u>.

<u>Jargon</u>: Use common sense. Read it aloud. If you stumble,
the line needs to be simplified.

<u>Spelling it out</u>. If a character spells out a word or a number, separate the elements with hyphens. For example:

                    BILL
          My name is Bill. That's B-I-L-L. I
          Ring Buzzer 60, that's six-oh.

<u>Shouting</u>. Use caps to indicate that a character is shouting. For example:

                    BILL
          No, listen carefully, the name is
          BILL!

<u>Whispering, crying</u>: Use parentheticals to indicate how a person is saying a line. Don't be too specific -- actors will make their own choices. For example:

                    BILL
              (quietly)
          Goddamned idiots, I hate ordering
          from there.

CHARACTER SLUGS:

<u>Keep character slugs consistent.</u> If a character is slugged ROBERT SMITH the first time he speaks, he must always be slugged ROBERT SMITH.

This rule includes characters who are identified by function; e.g., SGT. SMITH. If you slug Sgt. Smith as SGT. SMITH the first time, you have to re-slug him as SGT. SMITH, not SERGEANT SMITH or ROBERT SMITH or SMITH.

<u>Voice-over</u>. Use Voice-over in the following situations:

To comment on events: As in <u>Goodfellas</u>, when the narrator is reflecting in the past tense on events that are happening on-screen. Usually, narrators speak in the past tense.

To tell us what the character is thinking: As in <u>Dune</u>, when characters are telling us what they're thinking about <u>while</u> something is happening on-screen. The difference between this and the previous usage is that the narrator is speaking in the present tense.

When intercutting: As in <u>The Grifters</u>, when you're intercutting between what person A is saying in one scene and what person B is doing in another scene. The purpose here is to thematically link the two scenes.

If a character is speaking in voice-over, indicate it by putting (V.O.) next to their character slug. For example:

                    BILL (V.O.)
          I just knew from that day forward
          that danger was my beer.

<u>Point of View (P.O.V.)</u>: The proper syntax is:

P.O.V <u>SUBJECT</u> ON <u>OBJECT</u>

For example:

P.O.V DANNY ON FLAKE

P.O.V should always go on its own line and should always be in all caps.

<u>Off screen</u>. If a character is not visible but is in the
location, use (O.S.) next to their character slug when he
or she speaks. A good use of this is when a character is
in the next room of an apartment, or just went behind a
changing room partition. For example:

                    JACK (O.S.)
          I'm in the can.

Appendix

Appendix

A. Genre Articles

Genre Articles

Article 1

Hollywood Scriptwriter, June/July 2005

How to Understand and Apply Genre to Sell Your Screenplay with Ease

By Marilyn Horowitz

A producer once said, "No matter how good the story is, the first thing I think about is, how do I sell this?" To him, a screenplay was something to sell, so his first job was to figure out what sort of script he had so he would know to whom he could sell it. The next question was "How does a writer sell something to you?" He said, "I need to know what genre it is, you know, a thriller, a comedy or a drama."

Think about selling your screenplay as though you were selling a bottle of fine wine. All wine comes in a bottle and has a label that tells us not only what we will be drinking, but what kind it will be: red, white or rosé—which is what genre will help you do with your script. If you go into a liquor store, that's pretty much how wine is organized, and like a fine wine, your screenplay has to be presented in a way so that a producer can understand what he or she is buying. Genre can help you sell or finance your screenplay because your screenplay is a product like any other.

Genre, a French word from the 1770's, originally meant "sort, style, type," and later came to America in the 1920's and meant "having popular appeal." It's the style and the way a story is told that defines what we think of as "genre films." While most screenplays have elements of different genres, usually the script is more or less a thriller, a romantic comedy or a horror movie, etc. There are subgenres that can help you further define your script, such as "dramedy"—a drama with jokes, and "black comedy"—a comedy about a dark subject. We understand things by comparison and contrast. A script that has big action sequences is more like an action movie and less like a drama. Genre helps us understand and describe that distinction with ease.

Each genre has its own conventions. The Action movie has good guys, bad guys and a battle to be won. A Romantic Comedy has two people who somehow must get together and find true love.   And a horror movie has people terrorized by evil.   Classic examples are respectively *Die Hard, When Harry Met Sally* and *Scream*.

While genre provides a set of rules for each type of story, this seeming limitation sets the writer free, because once you know the rules, you can break them. Classic examples of successful films that have recombined typical elements of genre include *Married to the Mob*, a romantic Comedy/Gangster mix, *Blade Runner*, a Noir/Science Fiction blend, and *Ghostbusters*, a Comedy/Horror romp. Because the films were original ideas that incorporated recognizable genre elements, they could still be successfully marketed.

Genre is also a way to identify what kind of emotional experience you want your audience to have. For example, if you're intending to write a straight horror film, you want to scare your audience. But very often, you also want to include some funny dialogue. The question then becomes how to design your screenplay so that the audience will laugh only at your funny lines, not when the monster starts shredding people. Studying the elements of both horror films and comedies will help to organize the order in which the scary stuff and the jokes are placed in the story as well as what kind of plot to pick, so the first draft will have a good shot at being structurally sound. Understanding genre is the fast track to understanding structure, and screenwriting is all about structure. Each genre has its own variation of basic three-act structure. I tell my students that the goal is to study the genre they have chosen and then transcend it, because their work will be compared to everything that has been written before in that style. Once the student has determined which genre or genres will provide a basic template to build his or her story upon, he or she can then design an original story with just enough of the recognizable elements so that the story can be marketed and sold. Certainly a film like *The Matrix* has a complex spiritual agenda, but it is presented as an action movie. *The Upside of Anger* is a drama with jokes, or maybe a dark comedy, but it is really a mythic story of love overcoming all.

Genre is also a great tool when rewriting a screenplay. For example, if you've written a comedy and it just isn't funny enough, you may compare your story to other comedies and realize that the events you have chosen are too serious for the genre, so maybe you need to take out the double murder and replace it with a double cream pie in the face.

If the plot feels too predictable, you can go back and look at classic versions of your story and see what kinds of twists and turns they were using 20 or 30 years ago and see if there isn't a plot twist you can borrow and update. Mark Twain complained that "The Greeks stole all my good stories," so you certainly may turn to the classics for inspiration.

Using genre is the fastest way to design, write and sell your scripts. In my next article I will explore the elements of the basic genres and how to combine them to create new and original screenplays.

Copyright © 2005 Marilyn Horowitz

Article 2

Hollywood Scriptwriter, August/September 2005

How to Use Genre to Make Your Screenplay "Original"

By Marilyn Horowitz

A famous poet said, "If they haven't seen it before, it's original." But of course, there is little that is original and the question becomes how to tell your story in a way that seems new.

The previous article explored how to use genre to market your screenplays. In this article, we will identify basic genres and show you how to combine them to improve your screenplay.

Understanding the relationship between basic three-act structure and genre is the key. The easiest way to think about three-act structure is to break the 3 acts into four 30-minute sections and assign each 30-minute chunk a portion of the hero's journey. Act 1 becomes "Setting up the Dream"; Act 2, Part 1 becomes "The Hero's Nightmare"; Act 2 Part 2 becomes "Who or What Would the Hero Die for?"; and Act 3 is "The Resolution of the Dream."

For example, in the classic film *Witness*, Act 1 is about a cop, John Book, wanting to solve the murder of a fellow cop. Samuel, the young son of a widowed Amish woman, is the only witness. Book's dream is to be a good cop, but discovers that his own boss may be involved in the murder. When Book tries to investigate, he's shot. Act 2, Part 1 is his nightmare: he is wounded, trapped with the Amish, and unable to do anything. In Act 2, Part 2, Book falls in love with Rachel, but realizes that if he gets involved with her, he will have to stay in her world. He's willing to give up true love to solve the case. In Act 3, he resolves the dream by bringing his boss to justice. With this paradigm in mind, let's look at genre.

Below is a list of the basic genres, and some examples of how they have been successfully combined. Each genre has subgenres but to keep it simple let's use 12 genres and their basic plots.

<u>The 12 basic genres</u>:

Action/Adventure/Disaster: basic plot concerns physical force used to resolve conflict.

Comedy/Black Comedy/Romantic: conflict causes laughs.

Coming of Age: character must find place in society.

Crime/Police/Noir/Heist: a crime is committed and must be solved.

Epic/Myth: conflict takes place during great world events.

Fantasy: conflict resolved in real and imaginary worlds.

Gangster: gangster versus society.

Horror: monster must be defeated.

Love: two people want to be together.

Science Fiction: conflict set in a futuristic world with futuristic devices.

Drama: serious conflict between personal dreams and society.

Thriller: innocent hero/heroine must overcome homicidal villain.

<u>Movies with combined genres</u>:

Drama + Crime = *Witness*

Drama +Romantic Comedy = *As Good As It Gets, Something's Gotta Give*

Drama + Epic = *Gladiator, The Godfather*

Coming of Age + Action/Adventure = *Spider-Man 2, Batman Begins*

Coming of Age + Black Comedy = *Garden State, Adaptation*

Comedy + Gangster = *Pulp Fiction, Married to the Mob*

Comedy + Horror = *Ghostbusters, Shaun of the Dead*

Sci-Fi + Horror = *Constantine*

The way to combine structure and genre to "originalize" an existing project that doesn't seem "to pop" is to begin by identifying what genre your screenplay is in now and adding elements of other ones to it. Basics are plot, character and story. Plot is what kind of story is being told, the characters are the people who are in it and story is the way it is told.

A good example of a plot is the crime plot: Cop catches Criminal or not; the main characters are Cop, Criminal, Cop's Partner and Girl, and the story often begins with the committing of a crime and ends with the apprehension of the criminal. *Witness* has a basic cop plot: John Book, a good cop called upon to solve a murder. All is routine until he discovers that his only witness is a small Amish boy, and that a cop may have committed the murder. He tells his boss, who warns him not to tell anyone else, and the next thing he knows, Book is shot at. He realizes that his witness and the boy's mother, Rachel, are in mortal danger, so he drives them to safety only to discover he has been shot and must recover.

If this were your screenplay you would soon realize nothing is going to happen until Book gets well and faces his enemy and exacts justice. What to do? Here's where combining genres could serve you. In the film, the writers added a drama to fill in Act 2, Part 1 and a love story to fill in Act 2, Part 2. Then Act 3 picks up where the cop plot stops and completes the journey. Here's what's original: the subplot becomes the plot of Act 2.

If you were doing this for your own script, you would follow these steps. Decide what genre your script is in and then consider what elements from other genres you could combine with what you already have. You would identify the basic elements in your script. If it were a crime drama, the basic plot is a cop catches a criminal and the main characters are hero/heroine, villain and partner/buddy/love interest. Next, break up your story into three acts using our four-part structure and place the various plot events where they may fit. For example, we saw that the cop story only fit into Act 1 and Act 3 of *Witness*. You will be able to identify what works and what doesn't. Pretend your script is about a good cop with a good boss trying to solve a murder, and he falls in love with a nice girl. This is already a combined genre piece, crime genre and love genre. It's well-structured, fits into the three-act structure, but doesn't feel exciting or new.

You could borrow from the noir genre and make him a bad cop with a bad boss who falls in love with a bad girl, and suddenly the story is a bit like *LA Confidential*. You could make the cop an FBI Agent trying to solve a gangland killing and add comedy and you might end up with something more like *Married to the Mob,* or add science fiction elements and have something more like *Blade Runner*. You might also flip the genders. Make the cop a female and you get something more like *The Silence of the Lambs*. Try various combinations and look for that moment when you sense you're onto something new and then go for it.

To recap: Define your screenplay's genre, analyze it using the four-part three-act structure, then try out elements from other genres to see how you can refresh and lift your story. The more fun you have the better the result will be.

Copyright © 2005 Marilyn Horowitz

Appendix

B. Additional Blank Deconstruction Charts
and Mythic Journey Map Worksheets

Creating Your Screenplay Using the Mythic Journey Map and the Three Levels of Conflict

Write Your Premise-Question Here:

Page / Sequence	10 min / "Ordinary World" What is the world of the story?	20 min / "Call to Adventure" What happens to get the story started?	30 min / "Refusal of the Call" How does the main character deny the need for change?
		ACT I	
Plot			
On-screen Relationships (Outer Conflict)			
Hero or Heroine's Needs (Inner Conflict)			
Villain's Needs (Societal Conflict)			

Creating Your Screenplay Using the Mythic Journey Map and the Three Levels of Conflict

	ACT II — Part 1		
Page / Sequence	40 min / "Meeting w/ Helper/Mentor" Does the main character meet a mentor?	50 min / "Crossing the First Threshold" Does the main character enter a new world?	60 min / "Tests, Helpers, Enemies" Who/what are the new friends and obstacles our main character meets?
Plot			
On-screen Relationships (Outer Conflict)			
Hero or Heroine's Needs (Inner Conflict)			
Villain's Needs (Societal Conflict)			

Creating Your Screenplay Using the Mythic Journey Map and the Three Levels of Conflict

ACT II — Part 2

Page / Sequence	70 min / "**Approach to Innermost Cave**" How do the stakes go up? How does this send the main character in a new direction?	80 min / "**Ordeal & Flight**" How do things get bad enough to create a crisis?	90 min / "**Reward**" How does the crisis cause the main character to change?
Plot			
On-screen Relationships (Outer Conflict)			
Hero or Heroine's Needs (Inner Conflict)			
Villain's Needs (Societal Conflict)			

215

Creating Your Screenplay Using the Mythic Journey Map and the Three Levels of Conflict

	ACT III		
Page / Sequence	**100 min / "The Road Back"** What is the preparation for the final climax?	**110 min / "Resurrection"** How does the main character change?	**120 min / "Return w/ the Elixir"** What is the final showdown? Does everyone live happily ever after or not?
Plot			
On-screen Relationships (Outer Conflict)			
Hero or Heroine's Needs (Inner Conflict)			
Villain's Needs (Societal Conflict)			

The Mythic Journey Map Worksheet

ACT ONE:

1. What is the world of the story?

2. What happens to get the story started?

3. How does the main character deny the need for change?

ACT TWO:

4. Does the main character meet a mentor?

The Mythic Journey Map Worksheet

ACT TWO (Cont'd):

5. Does the main character enter a new world?

_____
_____
_____
_____
_____
_____

6. Who/what are the new friends and obstacles our main character meets?

_____
_____
_____
_____
_____
_____

7. How do the stakes go up? How does this send the main character in a new direction?

_____
_____
_____
_____
_____
_____

8. How do things get bad enough to create a crisis?

_____
_____
_____
_____
_____

The Mythic Journey Map Worksheet

ACT TWO (Cont'd):

9. How does the crisis cause the
    main character to change?

    _____

    _____

    _____

    _____

    _____

    _____

    _____

ACT THREE:

10. What is the preparation for the
    final climax?

    _____

    _____

    _____

    _____

    _____

    _____

    _____

11. How does the main character
    change?

    _____

    _____

    _____

    _____

    _____

    _____

12. What is the final showdown?
    Does everyone live happily ever
    after or not?

    _____

    _____

    _____

    _____

    _____

    _____

Bibliography

Bibliography

Aristotle, *Poetics*. New York: Hill and Wang, 1991.

Arnheim, Rudolph, *Visual Thinking.* Berkeley: University of California Press, 1971.

Ball, William, *A Sense of Direction*. New York: Drama Book Publishers, 1984.

Brande, Dorothea, *Becoming a Writer*. New York: St. Martin's Press, 1981.

Campbell, Joseph, *The Hero with a Thousand Faces*. New York: Princeton University Press, 1973.

Campbell, Joseph, *The Power of Myth.* New York: Anchor Doubleday, 1988.

Cameron, Julia, *The Artist's Way*. New York: G.P. Putnam, 1992.

Cameron, Julia, *The Vein of Gold*. New York: Jeremy P. Tarcher/Putnam, 1996.

Egri, Lajos, *The Art of Dramatic Writing*. New York: Touchstone/Simon & Schuster, 1960.

Field, Syd, *Screenplay: The Foundations of Screenwriting.* New York: Dell Publishing, 1994.

Ehrenzweig, Anton, *The Hidden Order of Art*. London: University of California Press, Ltd., 1967.

Gendlin, Gene, *Focusing*. New York: Bantam Books, 1978.

Goldberg, Natalie, *Writing Down the Bones*. Boston: Shambhala Publications, 1986.

Hamilton, Edith, *Mythology.* New York: Mentor Books, 1973.

Hicks, Esther and Jerry, *Ask and It Is Given*. California: Hay House, 2004.

Jung, G. Carl, *Man and His Symbols*. New York: Dell Books, 1968.

Klauser, Henriette Anne, *Writing on Both Sides of the Brain: Breakthrough Techniques for People Who Write*. San Francisco: Harper Collins, 1986.

Mamet, David, *On Directing Film*. New York: Penguin Group, 1992.

May, Rollo, *The Courage To Create*. New York: Norton, 1975.

McKee, Robert, *Story*. New York: HarperCollins, 1997.

Miller, Alice, *For Your Own Good: Hidden Cruelty in Child-rearing and the Roots of Violence*. New York: Farrar, Straus and Giroux, 1983.

Rabiger, Michael, *Directing: Film Techniques and Aesthetics*. Boston: Focal Press/ Butterworth-Heinemann, 1997.

Rico, Gabriele Lusser, *Writing the Natural Way*. New York: St. Martin's Press, 1983.

Shurtleff, Michael, *Audition*. New York: Bantam Books, 1980.

Stanislavski, Constantin, *An Actor Prepares*. New York: Theatre Arts, Inc., 1936.

Sun Tzu, translated by Lionel Giles, *The Art of War*. New York: Dover Publications, 2002.

Watts, Alan, *The Book: On the Taboo Against Knowing Who You Are*. New York: Vintage Books, 1982.

Westin, Judith, *Directing Actors*. Studio City: Michael Wiese Productions, 1996.

Wilen, Joan and Lydia, *How to Sell Your Screenplay*. New York: Square One Publishers, 2001.

Ueland, Brenda, *If You Want to Write*. St. Paul: Graywolf Press, 1987.

Vogler, Christopher, *The Writer's Journey*. Studio City: Michael Wiese Productions, 1992.

Zinsser, William, *On Writing Well*. New York, Harper Collins, 2001.

Acknowledgements

Acknowledgements

Kashfiah Abdullah	Peggy Long
Lynda Barry	Donna Miller
Khris Baxter	Adam Moser
Ello Black	Adam Nadler
Arla Bowers	Martha Nochimson
Jafe Campbell	Richard Nochimson
Mick Casale	Amber Stogo
Aileen Crow	Mark Stogo
Terry Dolphin	John Tintori
Donna Flagg	Arthur Vincie
Gene Gendlin	Maureen Vincie
David H. Horowitz	Michael Zam
Diana Horowitz	All my students
Louise Horowitz	All my teachers
Roger Horowitz	Big Red Ram Das
Lapo Imelzi	Everyone at Wholesale Copies
Lea Kramer	Snowball
Michael Leluex	Those Who Watch Over Me